# GROWING UP DEAF

# GROWING UP DEAF

*Issues of Communication in a Hearing World*

*Rose Pizzo*
*(As signed in ASL to Judy Jonas)*

12580-PIZZ

To order additional copies of this book, contact:
Xlibris Corporation
1-888-7-XLIBRIS
www.Xlibris.com
Orders@Xlibris.com

# CONTENTS

To my family: Vincent, Nancy, Karen and Paul.
Also to Linda, my daughter-in-law, who inspired
me to tell my story for my grandchildren, Michelle,
Vinnie and Dominic.

# INTRODUCTION

Many years ago, Vincent and Rose Pizzo, a Deaf couple, were visiting their Deaf friends, Ruth and Jimmy Stern. The Sterns had a book about Jimmy's hearing grandfather. He heard about a mother and two daughters detained at Ellis Island because they were Deaf. As the son of Deaf parents, Jimmy's grandfather was sympathetic, went to the authorities and said he would be responsible for them. The idea of a life story, about a Deaf family, fascinated Rose. It planted a seed in her mind. Maybe, someday, she would tell her life story to somebody who would write it. However, it didn't happen for a long time.

Linda, Rose's daughter-in-law, was fascinated with Rose's Deaf experience and by Deaf culture. She encouraged Rose to write about her life as a Deaf woman. Sometimes, Rose tried to write her life story, but writing English was a major struggle. American Sign Language (ASL) was her strength. English was her second language.

Rose had worked as a Teacher's Aide, at the Fair Lawn Deaf Program, in New Jersey, for twenty years. One of the founders of the program, Judy Jonas, had watched Rose's progress. In 1978 Rose was a motivated, but rusty student in the new Adult Basic Education (ABE) Program for the Deaf. She worked hard for her high school equivalency diploma and was then hired as a Teacher's Aide. She became a role model for many Deaf students trying to improve their English skills. In the mid 80's, she also became a Sign Language Instructor at the Fair Lawn Community School, in charge of her own class of hearing adults! What an amazing transition!

Over the years Rose and Judy became friends. In 1999 Judy

planned an early retirement from her 20 years as Co-Coordinator of the Fair Lawn Deaf Program. Judy had gone back to school and completed an Interpreter Training and ASL Deaf Studies Program. She had many plans: a second career as an American Sign Language—English Interpreter and directing a nationwide research project about Deaf people and their hearing siblings.

When Rose learned about Judy's plans to retire, she asked Judy to help write her "life story." Rose explained how she had tried to write on her own, but couldn't express herself well in English. They talked briefly about why Rose wanted to write her biography. Rose wanted her family to know about her life, understand her history and learn something about Deaf people. She was worried they wouldn't understand her life as a Deaf person. She wanted her three hearing children and grandchildren to know Deaf people were not just people who could not hear. She wanted them to know that, to her, Deafness was a culture with unique life experiences. Being Deaf affected every facet of her life. Her culture included a language, American Sign Language, which she shared with other Deaf people and with hearing people who knew it.

Judy didn't know how to say "no" to a friend in need. After working with Deaf people for more than 25 years, Judy knew that expressing themselves in English rather than ASL, was hard for Deaf people, including Rose. However, she also knew Rose's life story would be important and time-consuming work. She went into a full-blown panic. The last thing she needed was another project. She agonized how to respond.

Judy tried to persuade Rose to sign her story in ASL onto videotape. Rose rejected the idea. She wanted a "book" for her family to read, not a videotape with interpretation. They then agreed on how to proceed. Rose told her life story in ASL while Judy interpreted into an audiotape. This plan met both their needs. As a Deaf person, Rose could tell her story in her most comfortable language, ASL, while Judy could get many hours practicing the skill of interpretation. Then the tapes would be transcribed and Judy would edit them.

That was how it happened. They met weekly for over a year. As time went on, both looked forward to Rose's "life storytelling" sessions. Rose listed topics she wanted to cover. Every so often, Judy would ask a question that would lead Rose to a flood of childhood memories. Their friendship grew and was nourished by the bond developed when people share lives with one another.

# PREFACE (ROSE)

Linda, my daughter-in-law has encouraged me to put my life into words. It would be a way for my grandchildren to learn and understand how life was for me, growing up Deaf in a hearing world. She inspired me to take on this project.

I would like to express my gratitude to my very special friend Judy Jonas for taking on this special project for me. When I first approached Judy to ask her for her assistance in writing my life story, I did not realize how much time and effort would be involved. Her dedication, honesty and true friendship have made this experience special for me, and I will always be grateful to her.

*Rose Pizzo*

# PREFACE (JUDY)

This story has many facets. Let me explain.

*Interpretation and Trust Building*

First, this life story is an interpretation of a life story told in a language other than English. Rose told her life story in ASL and I interpreted it into English. That involved several challenges. Initially, Rose had her eye on me while I was interpreting. She wanted to lipread what I was saying. She knew, as many Deaf people have learned, that hearing people, even skilled interpreters, misconstrue what they sign in ASL. I understood her anxiety but I also became aware it was stifling her flow and interfering with her thought process. It took a while before she trusted me sufficiently to look past me, while she signed and I interpreted into a tape recorder.

*My Skills as an Interpreter were Repeatedly Challenged and Checked*

Even after trust was established, occasionally, Rose would want to check that I was understanding her ASL. Although I have worked with Deaf people for 25 years, I was new to interpreting as a professional. We both knew interpreting was a different skill from simply using ASL. She would stop and ask me "What did you say for all that?" I would stop the tape, rewind it, listen to myself speaking and sign to her exactly what was on the tape, word for word. Often Rose would beam. Her smile meant I had it right. We were both pleased. I was getting the interpreting practice I needed and Rose was telling her story!

*Rose Teaches Me ASL*

Other times Rose would use an ASL idiom and then stop and ask, "What did you say?" When I told her, she didn't always agree that my English expressed what she meant in ASL. I had missed the nuances of the ASL. She would keep giving me examples until I understood it to her satisfaction. Together, we would pick the best English equivalent for her ASL meaning.

### I Teach Rose English

Other times Rose would use a sign, and I'd stop the tape to point out I had about fifteen words in English that were equivalent to her sign in ASL. Frequently, she was shocked to learn about the variety of English choices available. Over time, Rose taught me ASL while I taught her English. What a team! What an incredible experience for both of us the telling of this "life story" had become!

### The Spoken Word is Different from the Written Word

Rose and I carefully read the first set of transcripts, which was transcribed word for word exactly as I had interpreted them. Rose agreed, for the most part, that my interpretation was correct and I had captured both her intentions and the facts of her story. I was so relieved. However, we both noticed it didn't read well. Some sections were repetitive, words and phrases kept reappearing and it just wasn't smooth.

### My Editing Dilemma—Whose Story is This?

The next hurdle was my struggle with the idea of editing. Should Rose "tell her story" exactly as I interpreted it? It was factually accurate but it didn't read well. We agreed part of the problem was I was a novice interpreter and wasn't taking advantage of the variety of ways to say things in English. I was taking her ASL too literally. For example, if I saw Rose sign, "Of course," that's what I said in English because it's the most common English word for that sign. However, I should have been varying my English choices, using synonyms like "naturally," "sure enough" or "as you might expect." My shortcomings as an interpreter were creating a dull life story.

I decided to keep the "original" transcripts of my interpretation but to do a major editing job. I then struggled to keep Rose's voice in the written version of her story and not have it sound like me. My natural writing style tends to be academic. I agonized about how to write Rose's story. Rose's ASL is eloquent. Her English, which is her second language, is adequate, but not at the same level as her ASL. Since this was "Rose's story," it had to be a story Rose could read and understand without struggling and, at the same time, not diminish her. I believe I have met that goal. Rose has read it, revised it in many places and is comfortable it's "her story."

*What We've Both Learned*

As we moved through the year, I realized how honored I was to "help write Rose's life story." Rose let me into her world of growing up Deaf in a hearing world. I became aware how every tale, every event, had a Deaf perspective, a Deaf twist, that helped define Rose's identity. This is what makes Rose's "story" unique. It is not the story of a bitter woman nor of an angry woman. It is not the tale of someone who "overcame obstacles" as a Deaf person in a hostile hearing world. It is the story of one woman, growing up Deaf in an Italian immigrant hearing family, in the twentieth century. It is the story of the two worlds she saw and navigated daily: Deaf and hearing. We see it from her eyes as a child. We see it from her perspective as mature wife, mother and grandmother. It is the story of many Deaf men and women of this past century. I'm delighted she asked me to help her.

One day I explained the meaning of the idiom "two way street" in the context that "Our weekly sessions had become a 'two way street'." She helped me learn her language and gave me a deep look into Deaf culture. I helped her tell her story. We both grew and we both gained what cannot be measured—friendship, trust, respect and love for another human being. For this I am grateful.

*Judy Jonas*

# CHAPTER 1.

## EARLY CHILDHOOD MEMORIES

**My Birth**

I was born on Easter morning 1932 with help from my Aunt Diana, known by her Italian name, "Titsi". Titsi has probably told me a thousand times, "I will never, never forget the day you were born," and then would tell me the following story. Mom's labor pains had started, but she didn't know how to contact the doctor. They didn't have a phone or a car. Somehow the doctor was contacted but he came to the house, told mom she was in false labor, and left. Mom again told Titsi, "The pain started again. I'm telling you. This baby is coming."

Pop raced out to catch the doctor. As they were running back to the house, a police officer saw the two men running and stopped them because he thought they were running away from something. They explained they were rushing home because mom was in labor. By the time the police let them go, I was already born and my aunt had helped mom deliver me. The doctor only cut the cord. Every birthday, my aunt reminds me of her important role in bringing me into the world.

**Moving from Manhattan to Staten Island, to Corona and to East Elmhurst**

I was born during the Depression. I have an older sister Frances, who was born 13 months earlier. Everyone called Frances "Cina," because they named her after pop's mother, my grandmother, Francesca, whose nickname was Cina. When mom and pop first came to America from Italy, they lived with my aunt and uncle on 47th Street and Second Avenue in Manhattan. Soon after I was born, we moved from the city to New Dorp, Staten Island because we couldn't afford the rent in Manhattan. We moved into Pepino and Titsi's large one family house along with their children, my cousin Frances and her brother Vincent.

Not too long after we moved to New Dorp, pop opened a business as a shoemaker in Jackson Heights, Queens. The commute from Staten Island to Jackson Heights was unbelievable. First he had to take the ferry, then he had to take the train. He got up in the wee hours of the morning and he didn't get home until 11:00 at night. He did this horrible commute every day and I know it was hard for him. My father was so exhausted from commuting, we moved to Queens, to an apartment in Corona. My brother Vincent was born there.

We didn't stay in Corona long. Pop bought a house in East Elmhurst on Humphrey Street where I spent most of my childhood. I loved the neighborhood. It was a beautiful tree-lined street with lovely duplex homes, one next to the other. I was lonely as a Deaf person because I didn't have many hearing friends to play with me. Soon after we moved to Humphrey Street, Titsi and Pepino moved to a house on a dirt road right behind our house. Again we felt like "the family" was together.

Titsi was like a grandma to me. She was a dressmaker and she made sure my sister and I were always dressed well. For many years, she sewed all our dresses and suits for the holidays. Our families were close and we spent so much time together, it was like we were one family living in two houses! Of course, we always spent Christmas, Easter and Thanksgiving holidays together.

## My Complicated Family

l-r: pop (Settimo Infantino), Titsi, mom (Grace Infantino),
Pepino,

l-r: Rose, cousin Frances, my sister Cina, April 1945

I come from a complicated family because my mother's sister, Titsi, married my father's brother, Pepino. In those days, men and women didn't just fall in love and get married. Parents used a matchmaker to select an appropriate mate for their children. Titsi and Pepino's marriage was the result of the matchmaker's choice. But Titsi was lonely in America without any relatives. So Pepino sent his brother, my father, to Italy to marry and bring Titsi's sister, my mother.

Like many immigrant families, many older relatives had both English and Italian names. Diana was "Titsi" and her husband was "Pepino." Their children, my cousins, were "double cousins," because they were related to me through both my mom and pop.

If this isn't confusing enough, their daughter and my sister are both named Frances! Cousin Frances is about 10 years older than I. When my sister's children and my children were born, my sister decided the children should call our cousin Frances "Aunt Frances" instead of "cousin Frances." We were close as children and she (cousin Frances) was older, almost like a big sister to me. We also had many relatives in the family named Vincent, including cousins, uncles and my brother. The funny thing is, though, we never called my brother "Vincent." We used to call him "Vinner." We still do.

Our relatives came to visit often. Of course, I knew relatives by their faces, but I didn't know anybody's names. Even now, I don't know many relatives' names. I guess it's because I never used them. If I need to know the name of a relative, I have to ask one of my cousins! This is true of most Deaf people. They don't know many relatives' names because no one takes the time to tell them and they don't hear the names used.

In fact, Deaf people use name signs for one another and for hearing people too. Frequently a person's name sign describes something about a person's looks. It may be their hair, their eyes or perhaps the way they walk. Not knowing a relative's name was normal for me. Someone in the family would tell me a name. Then they would tell me the relationship to someone I knew, like, "That's Grace's mother" or "That's Anthony's father." The relationship was easier to explain than the long unpronounceable and hard to lipread names.

### Having My Tonsils Out . . . At Home and Became Deaf?

Recently I got a letter from my cousin Frances. I asked her to write to me because she's older and I knew she would remember things about me when I was little. One day in the fall of 1934, she came home from school at lunchtime and she smelled something horrible. She said I was laying in the middle of the round kitchen table with the doctor standing over me taking out my tonsils. The doctor then put my tonsils in a glass. I guess removing tonsils at home was common in those days. I don't remember a thing because I was only two years old. Frances remembered it very clearly. It made quite an impression on her!

My mom always felt, from the moment I was born, I was a weak, not 100% healthy baby and said I was often sick. For example, normal babies sit up, crawl and walk at different stages but I was late for all of them. When I was about 2—2 ½, I had many ear infections and colds. The doctor diagnosed it as tonsillitis. My mom and other members of my family think I became Deaf when I had my tonsils out. I was talking before I had the operation. According to mom, I was definitely a hearing baby. I used to sing. I used to react to the music of the ice-cream truck coming down the street. Soon after I had my tonsils out, whenever mom called me, I didn't turn around. I never heard her call me.

## Cousin Vincent

cousin Vincent

My aunt's son, Vincent, was my favorite cousin. He would always play with me and pay attention to me. I felt more connected with him than with many others in the family because he took such an interest in me. After my aunt moved out of our home into her own home, we saw each other often. Once we were visiting them. I saw my cousin Vincent lying in bed. I must have been around three or four years old at the time and Vincent was about twelve. He was lying in bed and I wanted to play with him and he said, "No." I didn't know he was sick. I don't think I even knew the meaning of the word "sick." I'm sure nobody told me he was sick. I was Deaf. I didn't have any idea what was going on.

A few days later, I went to my aunt and uncle's house. I was hoping to see Vincent again. I did see Vincent. He was lying in a huge box, surrounded by flowers and relatives crying. I remember going close and looking at him. He was quiet and looked like he was asleep. Then time passed and I kept waiting to play with him but I never saw him again. I kept waiting and waiting to play with him and thought he would come back. I expected to see him every time we went to my aunt and uncle's home, but, of course, he never came back. Nobody ever told me he died. The last time I saw him was at my aunt's home, at his wake.

## Mom Takes Me to Doctors And Hurts Herself

While I was growing up, mom took me to many different doctors to see if they could help me hear. I didn't have the foggiest idea what was going on. Mom would tell me we were going to the doctor and I just went. The doctors would stick head phones on me and I had to raise my hand if I heard anything. One doctor, a chiropractor, lived across the street from us on Humphrey Street. He told my mother that chiropractics could help me hear. Today we know it's ridiculous, but it's what he told her. I would have to lie down on his medical table while he did all kinds of weird things with my head. Of course, it wasn't successful but I did go often.

Once, after yet another visit to another doctor, I noticed mom looked incredibly sad. She seemed heartbroken and frustrated because the doctor couldn't "fix" my hearing or cure my deafness. I could tell from the expression on her face.

As we went down to the subway together, Mom started to fall down the stairs. I was probably about five or six years old and didn't know what to do. I ran down to where she had landed at the bottom of the stairs. I noticed a man walking toward us and hoped he would help. He didn't, but continued walking, ignoring us. The station was deserted, so mom and I just sat there, mom sobbing hysterically. We clung to each other and, eventually, with my help, she got up. I helped her into the train and we went home. We were unable to talk about what had happened but mom was limping. I remember feeling totally helpless because I couldn't help her and we couldn't communicate. Simple everyday communication was lacking because I was Deaf.

### Communication at Home

It's hard to explain how I felt as a Deaf child growing up in a hearing family. I felt like a normal happy kid in many ways. At home I was always curious about what was going on. I remember asking a million times, "What did you say? " Frequently, whoever I asked, didn't tell me much. It was too much trouble to tell me the whole story. I would get the abbreviated version like, "She hurt herself." I never got the full story or many details. I was lucky if I got a brief summary.

My sister and my cousin Frances say I was always "screaming." I remember screaming. At the time, I didn't understand why. Now I know it was from frustration. I wasn't aware I had so little communication. I was interrupting them, to find out what they were talking about. I would interrupt asking, "What did you say?" They would answer, "Later. I'll tell you later. Just wait a minute." They saw my interruptions as constant "screaming for attention." As a kid, it's true, I was always "screaming" for information or interrupting, because I was left out of their conversations. Now I see we had entirely different perceptions of my behavior.

### Pop Forgets Pepino

Every morning, pop drove me to Roosevelt Avenue in Corona. There I waited for the school bus to P.S. 47 in Manhattan. Pop also drove Pepino to the nearby elevated train. We had the same routine every morning. Pop would start the car, I would get into it and Pop would back the car out of the driveway onto the dirt road. Pepino would drop his lunch in the car, then go back and close the garage door. Finally, Pepino would get into the car and we would drive to the bus stop and the elevated train.

One morning, a strange thing happened. Picture this. I'm sitting in the car, waiting for Pepino. He comes over to the car, drops his lunch, and goes back to shut the garage door. Pop, thinking Pepino is back in the car, takes off. Pop's driving along and I'm trying to get his attention to tell him Pepino is not in the car. Pop is totally ignoring me or doesn't understand me. I'm tapping him on the shoulder, "Papa, Papa." Communication was a disaster between us. I didn't know what was going on. Maybe pop thought it was supposed to be that way. We get to Roosevelt Avenue and my father finally notices Pepino is not in the car. It was one of the weirdest things that ever happened to me. I tried hard to tell pop that Pepino was not in the car. What did he do? He ignored me or didn't understand what I was trying to say. To this day, I don't even know whether pop went back to get Pepino or not. I just took my bus to school.

**Vacation Memories**

When we were kids, the family never took vacations together except to stay with relatives. My favorite childhood memories are of our visits to Titsi and Pepino's summer home in New Dorp, Staten Island. We stayed there for the whole summer, Fourth of July through Labor Day. I cherish those memories. From their home we could walk to the beach, so it felt like a real vacation.

I always looked forward to New Dorp. The kids out there were extremely friendly. I eagerly looked forward to seeing them and they looked forward to seeing me. They talked with me and played with me. The kids there always included me and I was just part of the group. It was not like the kids in East Elmhurst. I couldn't make friends in my Queens' neighborhood but I did in New Dorp.

I think I now understand why. A Deaf couple lived nearby who ran a hardware store in the neighborhood. Maybe the kids had figured out how to interact with them. I used to see them signing together in the store but I don't remember signing with them. I was very young at the time. I was afraid of them and didn't talk with them. Maybe through experiences with them, the neighborhood kids had learned how to communicate with Deaf people. It's possible their experience with this Deaf couple helped me have hearing friends during my summers in New Dorp. I'll never know the reason but I do know I have warm memories of those summers.

Another time mom took me, my sister and my brother to my mom's aunt and uncle's farm in Pennsylvania. Pop didn't go. He stayed home and worked. It was quite a trip from Queens. I remember we took a bus and had to sleep on it overnight. Mom's aunt was a sweet old lady. She let me play at milking the cow and I can remember seeing, for the first time, chickens laying eggs. It was a wonderful place. Mom's aunt would make home made rolls which my sister and I gobbled down on the bus ride home.

**Special Prayers for Me—"Our Lady of Mt. Carmel"**

Every year mom took me to a religious festival in New York to pray for me to hear. I wasn't aware of it, but my sister Cina says it's what happened. Our family belonged to Saint Gabriel's church in East Elmhurst where I had my communion and my confirmation. The priest told all of the children they could pray for a special novena, anything they wanted. I was there, too, but I never understood him. Mom told my sister to make a novena for me to hear. Cina says she would frequently make that novena.

Once my sister asked the priest, "How come my sister Rose can't hear? I've done this novena for her for a long time." The priest told my sister, "There is going to be another special way, a special way for Rose." Cina believes the special way did happen. The special prayer, the special novena that came true, was my marriage to Vincent at Saint Gabriel's church. My family adored Vincent. He was handsome, he was lovable and he loved me. Cina finally realized the answer to her novena was my marriage to Vincent and our wonderful children. Those were the answers to my sister's novena. Cina also believes that all I have accomplished, such as teaching and helping hearing students understand Deaf culture, were another special way God found for me. She always calls me the "star" of the family.

**Christmas at Home**

Christmas in our home was always a special event. When I

was a little girl, pop would always play Santa Claus but, like
most kids, I didn't know it. We had a tradition about Santa Claus.
I was always excited when Santa Claus was in the house but it
was weird, because when Santa Claus left, pop would come home
with Italian bread. It was odd because I would say, "Pop, pop,
you missed Santa Claus. He was here." Pop would say, "Well, I
had to go to the store and get bread. I'm sorry I missed him."
This went on for years. You'd think I would put it together, but
I didn't. I just never made the connection pop was Santa Claus.
As we got older, of course, we didn't have Santa Claus anymore.
As my younger cousins came along, we had Christmas with the
family and then we had Santa Claus again.

# CHAPTER 2.

## MY EDUCATION: INTRODUCTION TO THE DEAF WORLD

### School Days

When I was old enough to be starting school, I first went to hearing school. Mom and pop didn't know anything about Deaf schools so they sent me to the hearing elementary school, near home. I sat in the back of the classroom, and didn't learn a thing. I didn't make any friends because I was totally unable to communicate with the other children. I tried to pay attention but couldn't understand what was going on. It's hard to explain what it was like in those years in the hearing school. I was desperate for attention. I kept saying to people, "What? What did she say? What did you say?"

All of my classmates went on to the next grade, every one of them, but I just sat in the same grade for two whole years. At the end of school day, I walked home but the kids would pick on me, punch me and tease me. They did it every day. Most days, I sobbed all the way home. Finally, my mother spoke to the teacher and told her the children were picking on me. The teacher finally agreed to keep me in school until the other children left. Then I would leave and walk home alone.

### P.S. 47, 23rd Street Deaf School—Learning to Sign, Making Deaf Friends

One of my mom's Italian neighbors, who owned a store, had a deaf son. This neighbor told mom about a school for the Deaf, P.S. 47 on 23rd Street. The first day I went to school I was stunned. I saw all these Deaf children signing to each other. Somehow, even though I didn't know how to sign, from that day, I became a person who could understand things, someone who loved school and loved to learn. It was the beginning of my life as a Deaf person.

Strange, but I could understand the teachers though they didn't sign. They spoke. Somehow they knew how to communicate with us in a way other hearing people couldn't. Everything was oral. In the classrooms, we wore head phones and we had to speak and lip read. The teacher would talk and we would try to listen through these head phones. We didn't hear any words. We would just hear noises. Using signs was forbidden in the classrooms, but everywhere else, in the halls or bathrooms, we signed. They couldn't control those places! Sign language was officially forbidden, but I learned to sign at P. S. 47! Somehow American Sign Language (ASL) was just our natural language and we all learned it from each other.

When I started at P.S. 47, we called it "The 23rd Street Deaf School." I have a strong memory of my first day of school there. I was happy. I was excited to go to a Deaf school. At home, communication was difficult. I had no friends in the neighborhood, only my sister's friends. Once I went to the Deaf school, I developed my own friends. I adored being there. I felt like a happy, confident person and I was learning. As I got older, I became a leader in school. I loved the teachers too.

I felt like I almost had two different lives. At home, my sister was overprotective of me. Mom was always telling her, "Watch Rose! Watch Rose! Take care of her." While we were growing up, my sister had to defend me a lot. Looking back, I feel both my sister and my family took care of many things for me. However, at school, I could stand up for myself and be an independent person.

My first grade teacher, Mrs. Crandell, was my favorite. I had no problems understanding Mrs. Crandell. To this day, I still remember her. She was a tiny little lady, meticulous about everything. My most vivid memories about school are from our speech lessons. I remember the mirror. Mrs. Crandell and I would sit in front of the mirror and practice speech. She would help us feel the "m" or the "n" on the nose. For certain sounds, like a "b" or a "p" we would hold a piece of paper in front of us. If I pronounced them correctly, the paper would move. I found these lessons interesting and have wonderful memories of Mrs. Crandell and her speech lessons.

When I look back at my school years at P.S. 47, I know I loved all of my teachers, every one of them. Maybe because I was just happy there. For me school was like a second home.

### Neighborhood Friends

When I was a child, I would often look at my sister and brother, who each had many friends in the neighborhood and wished I could, too. Our lives were quite different. I had no neighborhood friends. Not even one. I lived in Queens but went to school in Manhattan and all of my friends lived in different boroughs all around the city. Some lived in Brooklyn, some in Queens, others in the Bronx or Manhattan. Since I lived in Queens and my school was in Manhattan, I had to get on the school bus right after school and go directly home. My school did not have after-school activities like schools have now. The only way I could see my friends was on weekends. When I was younger, before I could travel the busses and trains on my own, summers were the worst. I had no friends in the neighborhood. None. Nobody just to hang out with. Most of the time I'd go to pop's store and help him in his shoe shop.

### Helping Pop in the Store

Every Saturday, when my sister and I were little, we would go to pop's store. We would dress up in our finest clothes and help him clean the store, bathrooms included! Odd, but mom would always make sure we were dressed in good clothes, even though we were cleaning and working in the shop. When we were older, we didn't wear such fancy clothes, but we did continue to help pop in the store.

I spent most of my summers helping pop. Summers were hard for me. My Deaf friends lived all over the city; visiting them was hard because I was too young to travel alone on subways or buses. So during the summer, I would ride my bicycle to pop's store. My dog Nellie sat in the basket, on my handlebars, riding along with me. Nellie could have jumped out and killed herself but I never thought it was dangerous. I felt like I was Dorothy in the Wizard of Oz riding around with her in my basket. It took about an hour to bike from East Elmhurst to Jackson Heights. I just rode happily along with Nellie in my basket. This shows how independent I was as a child. My parents didn't hover over me. They trusted me. It's probably why I'm such an independent person today. I had a tremendous amount of freedom to go and do things on my own. I thank my parents for that.

When I finally got to pop's store, I did a variety of things. When I was little, my sister and I mostly cleaned. As I got older, pop taught me how to use some of his equipment. For example, pop would put on new heels, then I would use a machine to polish, buff and smooth them. Polishing wasn't my favorite task, but I knew I was helping. Once I had the most horrible experience. I was buffing the heel on a shoe and a strap broke on the machine. My face was covered with black gook. Pop thought the whole thing was hysterical and couldn't stop laughing. He knew I was there to help him and it was an accident.

So I spent my summers helping pop and becoming a shoemaker. Frankly, I had nothing else to do in the summer with my time, so I was willing to go every day. If the weather were nasty, I wouldn't take my bike and Nellie; instead I would take the trolley.

Most people don't realize that, unlike most hearing kids, during the long summers I could hardly wait to get back to school. I knew I had more communication and socialization at school with my Deaf friends, and eagerly looked forward to starting school again in September. One winter, when I was around nine years old, they canceled school because of a blizzard. At the time it felt like torture because I desperately wanted to go to school. This is true. I spent the whole day sobbing because school was closed. I kept whining, "I want to go to school."

**Learning My Name**

My sister, who is 13 months older, had to take care of me all the time and watch me. It may be strange, but she never called me Rose. She would call me "Baby." "Baby." I was only 13 months younger than she, but the name stuck. The whole family called me "Baby." Everybody, including me, thought it was my name. Members of the family would say, "Baby did this. Baby did that." Even my sister's friends called me "Baby."

It's scary when you think about it. I didn't know my name was "Rose" until I went to the Deaf school, P. S. 47. I was already eight years old! The school taught me my name! At the hearing school, I didn't know my name. It's the truth. Before I went to the Deaf school, I was totally isolated. Things changed after I began school with other Deaf children.

**Occasionally I Fought Back**

I'll never forget when I did a mean thing. Maybe I was getting back at some things that had been done to me. One day, when I was about eleven or twelve, I was thinking about my sister's friends. I often felt inferior to them. They looked so cool. This particular day, I did an awful thing and I have no idea why I did it. A girl lived across the street. She wasn't even my sister's friend. She was just a neighbor. I just remember feeling so furious, I threw a rock at her. There wasn't any reason to throw anything at her. We weren't even fighting. The stone hit her in the forehead and the blood came spurting out. After that, I have a feeling the family thought I was mentally retarded.

Looking back, I think this was the way I was expressing my frustration. However, at the time, I didn't even know her well enough to throw a stone at her. Maybe I was just getting back at hearing people. I couldn't use words to insult them and I couldn't deal with them verbally so I just threw things.

### Pop Worked Long Hours

Pop worked incredibly long hours. He left home at 6:30 in the morning and often did not get home until 10 or 11 o'clock at night. When he got home, he'd eat dinner all by himself. Most of the time I would give him a kiss "hello" during his dinner and say "Nite, pop." Then I would go to bed because it was my bedtime.

I had long days, too. First I got dropped off at Roosevelt Avenue. Then I would get the school bus to P.S. 47 in Manhattan. It would take an hour to get from Queens to Manhattan. When school was over, it was another hour back to Roosevelt Avenue where I had to take another bus to get home. My days were longer than most kids who walk two or three blocks to their neighborhood school. My cousin reminds me that often, after dinner, I would fall asleep at the table, I was so exhausted from all the traveling. It's common, even today, for Deaf children to have long commutes to and from the Deaf school programs.

### My Hands Were Slapped for Signing

As I said, P.S. 47 was an oral program. Although they did not allow us to sign in the classrooms, we signed in the halls and outside. Once I was in typing class and signed something to one of my friends. The teacher noticed, came charging over and smacked my hand with her pencil. I was stunned but continued typing. I knew they did not allow us to sign in class. The smack was my punishment. I had to respect the teacher. I thought it was okay. I wasn't upset.

Sometimes, the teachers would catch us signing. They would bang on our desks so we could feel the vibrations and their anger. They'd shout, "Stop signing. You have to talk. I know you can."

My friends and I just accepted it. We knew it was a hearing world and we had to learn to talk. We thought it was all right for teachers to yell at us for signing. We didn't think anything was wrong.

Now I look at what happened so long ago and I know it was wrong. The teachers didn't mean to hurt us. They deeply believed sign language would interfere with speech and lipreading skills. But lipreading was a constant struggle and we couldn't express ourselves well in speech. When they told us not to sign, it was like tying our hands. The thought of it just turns my stomach. I feel sad that it happened, but it did. However, times have changed. Today, P.S. 47 is a signing school.

**Explanations About Being Deaf . . . The Family Doesn't Sign**

Mom and pop never explained anything about my being Deaf but I knew I was Deaf. I remember feeling very frustrated and angry but I didn't understand why. I knew something was different. I knew I was happier at school but I never had the words to say, "I was happier in the Deaf World." I could understand the teachers. I could lipread the teachers. I could understand my Deaf friends. My teachers taught me how to lipread and speak.

I don't have a single memory of learning sign language. It seems like it was just my normal language. I don't remember how I learned it. I wish I could. I just remember signing. I've asked my sister why she never learned how to sign and I don't understand her answer. She said she can't do it. If she can play the piano then I don't know why she can't learn at least to finger spell.

# CHAPTER 3.

## ADOLESCENT MEMORIES

### My Dog, Nellie

brother Vinny and Rose (holding Nellie), about 1944

Growing up I had a dog named Nellie. She was an important part of my life. I adored her and felt a special bond with her. Nellie slept with me and we went everywhere together. I felt she was watching me and taking care of me. Somehow I felt Nellie knew I was Deaf and could understand me. For example, when somebody came to the house, Nellie would bark as if she were my hearing ear dog. That's what we would call her today. If people approached me, she would protect me. She would give them a look that told them to keep their distance.

I had Nellie for more than fifteen years. She was a Spitz: small, white and exquisite with a cute pointy nose and a gorgeous little face. She wasn't friendly with other people and most people were afraid of her, but she was tight with me. One time when she was old, she got sick. I knew she didn't have very long to live. I'll never forget one dark gloomy day when I was around sixteen. I was busy ironing, but Nellie was hobbling around, looking at me. I stroked her, then returned to my ironing and stroked her again. She had this strange way about her. The next thing I knew, she had fallen over. I didn't know what to do. I was screaming and sobbing, "Nellie, Nellie, Nellie." She had died right there in front of my eyes. It took me years to get over her death. She was the best pet I ever had. It was the first time anyone I loved had died. When my cousin Vincent died, I was too young to realize what was happening. Of course, after a while the pain diminished, but this dog was truly special to me.

**Time With Friends**

When I was in the fifth or sixth grade, I didn't have school busses taking me back and forth to school any more. I had to take the subway and a public bus to and from school. As I approached twelve or thirteen, I didn't go directly home anymore. When school was over, I would hang out with my friends at a park on Madison Avenue and 23rd Street. We played games, took pictures and just hung out together. Sometimes, seventeen or eighteen of us would be together in the park, especially in good weather.

As teenagers, we set up our own sports activities. On our own, kids from my school formed a team with Lexington School for the Deaf students, in Manhattan, on 67th Street. We had basketball and baseball competitions with a variety of schools:

the New Jersey School for the Deaf and hearing teams, too. We gave our baseball team the name, "Blue Swans."

As an adolescent, I traveled long hours to see my friends on weekends. I took the bus, then the train. Often it took an hour or more just to meet friends. Then, of course, we would do what teen-age young people do, hang out and chat. Sometimes we would go to the movies, foreign films with subtitles. After the movies, we had to go straight home before it got dark. We were only able to see each other for tiny little bits of time. It would take a long time to get home.

### I Learned to Sew

As a teenager, I didn't have many after school activities because I had to come home right after school. I used my free time to sew. I would get home from school, do my homework and then sew. First I would lay out all the material and the patterns and do all the pinning. The next day I would cut and sew. Gradually my closet became full of clothes I had made. I did all my sewing on mom's dining room table which Pepino made. His hand-carved table is still in my dining room. Some day I hope one of my children will want it so we can keep it in the family.

My sister didn't know a thing about sewing. After school she was with her friends who lived nearby. I couldn't be with my friends because they were scattered all over the city. So I sewed.

### Making New Friends—Deaf Friends from Deaf Families—A New and Different Perspective

As I got older, I started to make friends with some students from Lexington. I could travel busses and subways alone and could visit them in their homes. One girl, in particular, Anita, came from a Deaf family. Both of her parents were Deaf and she also had a Deaf brother. Her ability to express herself in ASL awed me. We would spend hours, like teenagers do, just chatting and laughing together. One day Anita invited me to visit and stay over, because I lived in Queens and she lived in Brooklyn.

Her house dumbfounded me! Her parents and her brother were all Deaf. The communication in her household was unbe-

lievable. Not only was her immediate family Deaf. They had
Deaf aunts, uncles, and cousins living downstairs. Deaf friends
would stop by and visit. Anita's uncle had a model railroad set up
in his apartment. We would go down and he would spend hours
explaining the trains in ASL. It was an amazing experience for
me to get lengthy explanations for everyday things in ASL. ASL
was everywhere in Anita's household. She had a Deaf world in
her home environment! I loved going there just to soak up the
ASL from her parents, relatives and friends.

What was also incredible about Anita's family was their sense
of humor. Everyone laughed constantly. Everything seemed hysterical to me. Watching her parents arguing would make me laugh,
I think because I could understand it. People were supposed to
argue but I had never seen adults arguing in sign language. I remember laughing so much because I had finally had access to
this regular, "normal family" stuff. Also, I remember feeling overwhelmed and impressed. Anita's father was a gentle, sweet man
who signed beautifully. I always told Anita she was lucky she
came from a Deaf family. When I was growing up, I always wished
I had a brother or a sister who was Deaf, like her. I was jealous.
We were friends for years and we're friends even now. My childhood memories of time spent with her family are precious.

Once when we were teenagers, we got back to her house
extremely late. Her parents were already sleeping and we didn't
want to wake them. But, as we came through the door, her mom
was standing there, waiting. She screamed at us and bawled us
out for getting home late. I had never seen anybody screaming in
sign language at their children and just stood there with my eyes
open wide. However, I was puzzled how her mom knew we
were home. I knew they were Deaf and couldn't hear us come in.
Her mom said to us, "What do you think I am, Deaf or something? I'm Deaf but I have a dog who lets me know when my
daughter comes home in the middle of the night! I may be Deaf
but I'm not stupid. My dog keeps me informed about what's
going on in this household!"

My parents didn't seem to understand Deaf people could be parents. I pleaded with mom to invite Anita and her parents for dinner. Finally, mom agreed. I thought mom and pop were being supportive and could hardly wait for Anita and her parents to arrive.

Sure enough, they came, but I was disappointed. My aunt and uncle joined us for dinner. Mom and pop spent the whole evening talking to them and totally ignored Anita and her parents. Deep inside I was mortified. I kept looking at mom and pop and then at Anita's parents. I didn't know what to do. They didn't interact at all! We all ate at the same table but my aunt and uncle were busy talking to my parents. Anita and her parents and I had a totally separate conversation in ASL.

I never talked about it with Anita until quite recently. We reminisced about old times, talked about the time we got home late and how her mom had yelled at us. We also talked about the evening her parents came for dinner. Her memories are totally the opposite of mine. Both she and her parents had a terrific time at our house. I said to her, "You know, Anita, I was disappointed that evening." She could hardly believe what I was saying and asked me to explain.

I explained the evening was a disaster for me because I felt caught in the middle between my hearing family and her and her Deaf parents. She was amazed at my perspective because she has warm memories of a wonderful evening when her family came to dinner. It proves how childhood perceptions of the same event can be quite different. We carry these memories with us into adulthood. I remember a separate Deaf and hearing evening where I felt caught between the Deaf and hearing worlds. She remembers a lovely evening where my close Italian family impressed her.

Looking back, I'll never know what would have happened if my aunt and uncle hadn't been there. Maybe mom and pop would have figured out how to communicate with her parents and maybe they wouldn't. Whether my memories would have been better or worse, I'll never know. It just didn't happen that way.

All these years, until I recently saw Anita, I was never quite able to express and discuss my disappointment about the dinner. I don't think I even had a way to express my feelings back then. I just kept everything in. I don't know why. I've spent most of my life keeping my feelings in. But I'm glad I've finally gotten it off my chest and had the opportunity to hear Anita's perspective.

### My Friend's Parents

When I was growing up, I would often go to my friend's houses. It's hard to believe, but some of their parents forbid us to sign in their homes. They would say, "You don't have to sign. You can lipread." Of course, we signed anyway, but we knew it was forbidden and did it behind their backs. My parents were just the opposite. Sometimes eight or nine of my friends would stay over and we would sometimes, like young people do, stay up all night happily signing away. My parents thought it was just fine. It never even occurred to them to stop us.

Imagine, my parents were Italian immigrants who were most comfortable speaking Italian. When the school told them they needed to speak English at home instead of Italian, they did it, so they would expose me to English. Yet they had no problem accepting our signing. The contrast in attitudes of my friend's parents and mine still puzzles me.

Once a friend invited me to her house. I didn't know her mother strongly opposed sign language. She was a firm believer in oralism, speech and lipreading. I recall signing with her daughter and the mother went into an absolute panic. She smacked my hands. I looked confused and my friend said, "I'm sorry. I'm not allowed to sign." I was in a total state of shock. She had never told me how her mom felt about sign. I know my friend was embarrassed. Soon after, our friendship diminished. After many years, we met again. Of course, she was using ASL. She told me her mom had died. I told her I was sorry and she just said, "That's O.K. I don't miss her at all." She had a miserable childhood.

Communication in her household was a disaster. The whole family's attitude toward sign language and toward Deaf people was negative. Occasionally, I had friends whose families were like that. She wasn't the only one. There were some that were against sign language. I felt sorry for them and am grateful my family was supportive.

I began to realize many of my friends did not come from homes as warm and loving as mine. I had four best friends in my life who came to my house regularly. They thought my parents were lovely and enjoyed my father's sense of humor. When I went to their houses, I found three had fathers who were alcoholics. I didn't even understand what it meant. I never saw my father drink, ever. My father was a hard-working man and when I look back on my family life, I realize my parents were special. They were poor immigrants, from Italy, who came to America to make better lives for themselves and for their family. I realize now they succeeded.

### My Deaf Friend, Betty Oshman Boosts My Confidence

My friend Betty Oshman is quite a bit younger but I knew her from school. Her parents were Deaf. Once they came to visit the school and she introduced me to them. I didn't realize it but she looked up to me as a role model. When she introduced me to her parents she said, "Mom and dad, I want to introduce you to my friend Rose. She is sooo smart. You would not believe how smart she is." I remember thinking, "Oh my God. She's talking about me." I could hardly believe it. Me? Smart? Impossible. I also felt flattered because, deep inside, I knew she was right.

### Arista . . . Graduation

In the seventh or the eighth grade, I received an honor society pin from the Arista Society. Hard to believe, but I saved the pin. Just recently, in 1998, I gave it to P.S. 47 for their archives. In those days P.S. 47 ended at the ninth grade, but now it goes through High School. On graduation day, I thought my heart would break. I was supposed to be happy, but I wasn't. None of us were happy because we knew that staying in touch would be hard. We didn't have TTY's back in those days. (A TTY is a piece of equipment that has a keyboard like a typewriter and it has a coupler for a telephone receiver. A deaf person uses the TTY with a regular phone and can have typed conversations with anyone else who has one. Today there are telephone relay services in every state, required by law, so that deaf people and hearing people can call each other. The relay operator reads the typing of the deaf person to a hearing person and then types what the hearing person says to a deaf person.)

Even though we planned to write letters or ask our parents to call for us, we knew how difficult having contact with each other would be.

P.S. 47 had a tradition that the girls make their own white graduation dresses. We all had the same corsage made of sweet peas. I had such mixed feelings as I marched down the aisle to get my diploma. I got so many awards at graduation, I was numb from the shock. I don't even remember what they were for but, definitely not English. Actually, I got the English award by mistake. Naturally, I thanked the person who gave it to me but wondered why I got it. Shortly after the ceremony, one teacher said to me, "I'm sorry. We made one mistake. Jane was supposed to get the English award. It was hers, not yours. You got it by mistake." I didn't complain or feel sad about it. I knew I shouldn't have won an English award!

**Gaining Self-Confidence at School**

Looking back, the reason I had friends at school and felt comfortable was that we could communicate. We shared our experiences and our stories. Truly, while I was growing up, there was a lot I didn't understand at home. But at school I could understand everything. Often the teachers would ask me to take on a leadership role. For example, once my gym teacher turned to me and said, "Rose, I need to leave for a few minutes. Would you come up here and lead the class in the exercises?" I remember thinking, "Wow. Me? Yes, I can do that. Imagine. She picked me!" There I was, leading the class, telling them what to do and showing them how. They all imitated me and did what they were supposed to do! I felt quite proud of myself. From experiences like this I began to develop self confidence and realized I could do things I never dreamed were possible!

I think school was the first place I had full communication. One year, maybe when I was fourteen, I was elected President of my class. I was in a state of shock over it. First, because they picked me and second, because I was the first girl ever elected as class President. I could hardly believe people would vote for me for President but they did. I can't even remember much of what I did as President but I recall thinking it was an important job. One of my responsibilities was to line up the children for various activities. I definitely felt important doing it. Now I'm the President of the Woman's Auxiliary and I have plenty of things to do! I could write a book just about that!

### Hearing Schools . . . Deaf Schools . . . There's a Difference

I remember one childhood experience when I went to a show at a hearing junior high school in East Elmhurst because a neighbor was in it. The show at the hearing school was a wonderful roller skating show. I was fascinated with the kinds of shows they had at the hearing school. I wished I could be part of that. I felt kind of separate. Of course. I was separate because I grew up in a school for the Deaf. But I was much happier in the school for the Deaf. We had shows at our school too. I definitely felt good when I was in them.

### Sweet Sixteen Parties

Once I was invited to one of my sister's friend's Sweet Sixteen party. All the girls, me included, wore long dresses. I remember sitting quietly, feeling like part of the wallpaper, because I didn't know how to be involved. I remember sitting there, in my long dress, watching everybody else chatting and dancing, the way teenagers do. I couldn't participate because I couldn't communicate with any of them.

When I turned "Sweet Sixteen" Pop gave me a Bulova watch that I still have to this day. For my party, I asked if I could invite my Deaf friends and if we could all wear long dresses like I had seen at my hearing neighbor's party. Of course, the answer was "Yes." We had the party at home and everybody showed up in long fancy dresses. That party, with my Deaf friends, leaves me with special, happy memories. What a contrast to the hearing party where I had felt isolated.

**Humphrey Street . . . My Hearing Boyfriends**

When we lived in East Elmhurst, Queens on Humphrey Street, the children in the neighborhood didn't have any way to communicate with me. One neighborhood boy, Tommy, who lived two doors away, was crazy about me. When I was about twelve or thirteen he said he was madly in love with me. It was so silly. It was the first hearing boyfriend I ever had. We spent lots of time together, but we just could not communicate. We would hold hands and smile at each other. Since he couldn't tell me himself he liked me, he asked my sister to tell me. After a while I got bored with him and wanted to break up with him. I couldn't tell him because I couldn't communicate with him. Naturally, my poor sister had to tell him for me! He was quite upset because he wanted to be my boyfriend.

A few years later, my sister was dating another boy named Tommy. One of his friends, Nick, wanted to date me. So the four of us double dated together. I wasn't thrilled about dating hearing boys because I was scared they would take advantage of me. I would never have dated him alone but felt safe with the four of us. The four of us would go to the movies together. In those days only foreign films had subtitles so we went to regular movies. Nick kept wanting to date me. Once, he came over to the house and he said to me, "I'm in love with you." He asked me to tell him how I felt. Just then a Deaf friend of mine showed up. Nick asked me, "Is he your boyfriend?" I answered, "Yes, he is." Poor Nick. He didn't know what to do. So he got up and left. That was the end of that. I never saw him again. I could see the hurt in his face when I told him this Deaf guy was my boy-friend but I didn't know any other way to end our "relationship."

About 15 years ago, I received a notice about a class reunion from my class at the East Elmhurst hearing school. Of course, I didn't want to go because it was a hearing thing, and I was Deaf. It just didn't feel like something I wanted to do. I didn't want to see my old hearing neighbors but my brother went and saw Tommy who asked if I were there. My brother told him where I lived and that I had a family. He was disappointed I didn't go. He had wanted to see me.

### The Strange Tale of Jimmy L.

Jimmy L. was one of my classmates at P.S. 47. He had Deaf parents and three Deaf brothers and was the youngest in his family. The older boys went to the New York School for the Deaf, known as "Fanwood," and the two younger ones went to P.S. 47, with me. I never understood why they went to different schools but I never asked them either. If I ever see them again, I will ask but, so far, I haven't had the opportunity.

Jimmy decided he wanted to join the army. Believe it or not, he passed their hearing test! He was 100 per cent hearing! He had grown up in a totally Deaf family with Deaf aunts, uncles and cousins. Somehow he went to a Deaf school but he passed the hearing tests and actually joined the army.

Looking back on this, I know the older two boys who went to Fanwood, were profoundly Deaf. Jimmy, the younger of two brothers, always said they were hard of hearing but it turned out Jimmy was hearing. When I used to go over to his house as a teenager, Jimmy would listen to the baseball games on the radio, and tell the family what was happening. I didn't think much of it at the time since I thought Jimmy was hard of hearing. Eventually Jimmy married a Deaf woman, which is not surprising since he lived in a "Deaf World."

### Thank You To My Parents

I am thankful my parents were concerned about my education and encouraged me to succeed in school. While I was at P.S. 47, the School for the Deaf, I saw kids coming into my Deaf school, for the first time, when they were already eleven or twelve year's old. Many were in a panic. Most had never seen signs before and they were frightened. Some had been hearing and suddenly became Deaf. Others were Deaf kids who had been kept in hearing schools and hadn't learned anything. Most never learned to sign well and many left school before graduation. They never learned any sign and never had any effective way to communicate.

It helped me appreciate my parents. They sent me young enough to learn ASL. My early experience at the Deaf school, P.S. 47, affected my whole life and helped me understand myself as a Deaf person.

My parents were also accepting of my Deaf friends. They didn't mind us signing. I remember seeing my friends with their parents who would say to them, "Read my lips. Don't sign with your Deaf friends. You can talk." My parents' open approach and open attitude toward me and my Deaf friends and their acceptance of our signing was a tremendous plus in my life.

I think the one thing I would want them to change, if they could, is to learn how to sign. Communication is so important. I would want them to have known my language. But looking back, at the time, they did not allow us to sign in school, though we all did. In those days, speech was the most important. My sister had to teach me speech constantly. It was all part of what we did. In school, we wore hearing aids, we had to listen and try to follow words. Things were very different from what happens in Deaf schools today. I wouldn't want to live through it again. I would want my parents to learn sign language so they could easily communicate with me. I want to add another thing. My family today, still says my speech is good because I had so much speech in my growing up years. I think I'm fortunate I have good speech and I'm a fairly good lipreader. I'm not sorry. I 'm not the least bit sorry.

### High School Years

When I left P.S. 47, again I went to a hearing school, Mabel Dean Vocational High School. Back then, P.S. 47's philosophy was that Deaf students must learn to fit in the hearing world. I thought I could do it. My high school was a mixture of academic and vocational training where I spent half a day at the academic high school and half a day at the vocational school. At first, everything was fine. I had one terrific teacher who would face me so I could lipread. I studied like crazy at home, and passed many tests. That teacher felt proud. She wanted to show everyone I could keep up with the hearing kids. I was proud of myself, too.

As I moved into the third year of high school, the teachers didn't seem to care about me or about my special needs as a Deaf student. Once there was a teacher I didn't like at all. I was sitting near a hard of hearing student. The teacher was talking non stop but I couldn't follow what she was saying. I didn't have the faintest idea what was going on but I saw her call my name, "Miss Infantino," two or three times. The next thing I knew, all of my classmates were staring at me, waiting for me to respond. I was humiliated. I'll never forget how upset I was. I don't even know if she was aware I was Deaf. I guess she must have known, but to humiliate me, in front of all my classmates, is an experience that has stuck with me all these years.

Most of the teachers at Mabel Dean High School refused to let me sit in the front of the room. They put me in the back of the room in any empty seat. As they talked, they would wander back and forth. It was impossible to lipread them with their backs turned. I was exhausted from trying to lip read all day long, I thought my eyes would fall out of my head. I told mom I wanted to leave high school and she said "No way. You absolutely have to graduate. You are not leaving high school."

After a while, I just couldn't stand it any more but mom wouldn't let me leave. Finally mom agreed I could switch to the vocational school full time and study dress making. I was happy and satisfied and enjoyed sewing. I still have my mom's sewing machine, but I don't sew any more. I'm too busy to sew, but it's funny. When I do sew, like if I fix a hem or something, I still enjoy it and I'm good at it. I know I sew well but don't have the time anymore. I'm too busy!

At my high school graduation I wore a cap and a gown but I didn't get a diploma. All I got was a certificate. I hadn't learned much. However, while I was in school, I made some good friends with those other hearing students. They were concerned about me and took an interest in me, especially one good friend, Theresa. She would sit next to me during tests and make sure I understood the questions. For example, in gym class I couldn't understand a thing the teacher said. Theresa would turn to me and say, "Did you understand what she said?" and if I said "No," she would explain everything to me. Amazingly, the teacher would punish her, for talking! The teacher was not aware Theresa was trying to help make sure I understood. Like most of the other teachers, she just didn't get it. She was totally unaware of, and no one helped her understand, my basic needs as a Deaf person.

Of course, back in the days when I went to Mabel Dean High School, there was no such thing as a sign language interpreter for Deaf students. However, P.S. 47 did send a teacher who was available in a separate resource room, in the high school, where we could go if we needed help. If we had a problem, we knew we could go and see Miss. Cleary. However, I didn't feel it was working. I never felt she could understand my problems because she wasn't in the classroom where the misunderstandings happened. She didn't see it.

What went on in that resource room was quite unbelievable. Miss. Cleary was never with us, in the classrooms, where we needed her. How could I explain events to Miss Cleary if I didn't understand them in the first place? It was the main reason I didn't finish the academic part of high school. I had Deaf friends who did put up with the academic classes. They tolerated four years of not understanding. They made their choice. I couldn't do it. I look back at the years I spent in high school not understanding and I'm glad I didn't go to the academic classes. I still wonder how my friends did it. They got the diploma and I only got a vocational certificate. At the time, I remember feeling jealous, but looking back, I'm not sorry. I could never have survived those extra classes.

Nowadays, it's just incredible. The interpreter is right there, in front of the class, with the teacher, for the mainstreamed students. It seems like a miracle to me. When I went to high school, we didn't have anything compared with what kids have today.

## My Jobs and More Schooling

When I finished high school, I looked for a job as a dressmaker. When I was growing up, Deaf women became dressmakers and men became printers. We didn't have the same goals as hearing kids and couldn't look for the same kind of job. My dream job was making bridal dresses but I just couldn't find anything. Eventually I found a job as a sewing machine operator. It was piece work. The faster you sewed, the more money you earned. It was a disgusting job and I hated it.

I did this piecework for about two years and despised every minute of it. Several of my Deaf friends were training to become key punch operators. Office work seemed terrific compared with piecework in a sewing factory. One of my friends suggested that I visit the school and observe. The place intimidated me. I was terrified. The teachers were talking and I didn't understand a word they said. However, I enrolled, worked hard and completed the training.

The first company I applied to hired me right away. The man who interviewed me had a blind daughter. I think he hired me because he was sensitive to people with disabilities.

# CHAPTER 4.

## SIBLING MEMORIES

**My Sister Frances**

l-r: Cina and Rose at communion, 1941

The best way I can describe my relationship with my siblings is to say that I'm Deaf and they're hearing. My sister and I are thirteen months apart. My sister called me "Baby" all the time because I was younger, not because I was a baby. My brother is the baby of the family.

I'd like to describe the way we communicated as children, but honestly, I don't even remember. I remember watching my sister talking. I do know I was very quiet. I also remember feeling very frustrated. I wanted to communicate with everybody, and I just couldn't. Like most siblings, my sister and I would argue. We would scream and yell, but in other ways we had a good relationship. We would disagree about whose turn it was to do the dishes or the cleaning. Nobody in my family signed, official signs, but we used homemade signs. When she talked to me, my sister always used her hands and made gestures. They weren't formal signs. She never did learn to sign.

My sister and I grew up almost as twins. Mom dressed us like twins, I guess, because we are only thirteen months apart. Naturally we didn't go to the same school because she went to a hearing school and I was in a Deaf school. It's hard for me to remember things that happened but I know we argued just like normal siblings. But I had a special weapon because I was Deaf. If we got into a huge argument and I didn't want to continue, I would close my eyes. It meant I won every argument because I could just withdraw by closing my eyes. My sister would have to stop. It gave me power, but, of course, I didn't think of it that way at the time. I just knew if I closed my eyes, I didn't have to "listen" to her yelling at me.

Looking back, I think my sister was terribly overprotective of me. I don't think she realized it at the time, of course. For example, my sister would yell at me. She would say "Be careful," and she'd grab me by the shoulders and say "Don't talk to strangers." She never took her eyes off me. If her friends were around, she was always watching me, like a mother hen. Now I understand she was trying to protect me.

I never felt bitter about the fact that my sister was hearing and I was Deaf. I never even thought about it. As a child, I felt lonely because she had friends in the neighborhood and I didn't. Still, my mom always made my sister take me along with her. She had to include me with her friends. But her friends and I didn't communicate. There I was, a "tag-along," but totally isolated. I don't know how she felt, but she took me. She just sort of accepted her lot in life.

My sister and I never talked about it. When my sister and her friends were planning what to do, I would stand there watching, like a zombie, not knowing what was going on. Her friends never talked with me. I was a good lipreader and I remember one of my sister's friends saying to her, "You **have to** take her?" My sister said, "Yeah, I'm taking her." Willingly. She didn't say it with anger. She just said, "Of course, I have to take her." My sister would just insist upon it. Maybe mom forced her to do it. I don't know why she did it. Her friends didn't want me tagging along with them but my sister always took me anyway, though I couldn't communicate at all. Those kids never even tried to communicate with me. Not a word. Not a thing.

I was stuck with my sister and her friends, and they were stuck with me, until I was old enough to travel on my own and visit my own Deaf friends from school. I traveled by bus or train to see my friends because they lived all over the city. Then, like most adolescent siblings, I was out of my sister's life and she was out of mine. Of course, at other times we were close friends. We are still close now.

### Her Friends Were Occasionally Mean to Me

Once I went to the store and one of my sister's friends came up to me. I didn't know how to respond because I was always afraid to talk to people. When my sister's friend approached, I was just about to say, "Hello," when this nasty brat stuck her tongue out at me. I was so hurt. "Why she would do that to me?" I wondered. Maybe because I was different or because she thought I was dumb. Maybe it was because I was Deaf. I had no idea what to do. I felt humiliated and just went home. I didn't even tell mom. I just kept it inside and didn't tell anybody.

Another time, my sister, her friends and I were riding bicycles near La Guardia Airport, near our home. A huge deep puddle was in the middle of the street. One girl never liked me. She said to my sister, "Why don't you push her in the water?" I didn't understand exactly what my sister answered but I saw her shake her head meaning, "No way. I won't do that." I remember it as an awful experience but at least they didn't push me in the water.

However, it goes deeper. I recall thinking that my sister's friend thought I was worthless and that my sister would better off if I were dead. I thought, at the time, it must be because I was Deaf. Fortunately, my sister didn't share her friend's feelings, but it definitely hurt me to know someone wanted to harm me and humiliate me.

**My Siblings and My Deaf Friends**

Mom warmly accepted my Deaf friends. They would often sleep over because they lived far away. Mom was wonderful about sleep overs. Sometimes, four, five or six girls would stay over. We would have so much fun at my slumber parties. They were frequently at my house because we had a big house and most of my friends lived in apartments. They loved coming over to my house and loved being with my mom. My friends didn't interact at all with my sister and brother. Not at all. My siblings avoided my friends, probably because they couldn't communicate. My brother and sister understood me but they definitely didn't understand my friends.

I always wished I had another brother or sister who was Deaf. I remember thinking about it often because communication was difficult between me and my hearing siblings. Especially, for example, if I would go to a wedding or a big family party, even as an adult. They always looked like they were having a good time while I just sat there. At best, I would have the most superficial brief conversations like, "How are you?" "Fine." "Children well?" "Yes." The end.

## My Sister Became My Tutor

Mom never used the term Deaf. She would say I was hard of hearing. When I started at the Deaf school, I was forced to wear hearing aids. At home, my sister had the job of helping me learn to use my hearing, although I was Deaf. She would say a color or a number behind my back and I had to pick the correct match for her word. These "lessons" were horrible experiences. I couldn't stand trying to make sense out of these noises. Once I just couldn't take it anymore and I just totally gave up.

## My Sister and the Piano

I always felt proud of my sister when she played the piano though I couldn't hear it. For example, when the relatives visited our house Sunday afternoon, mom would ask my sister to play the piano. The whole family sat and listened. I sat there, too, listening with my eyes and watching her. I wished I could play the piano. I was fascinated by her body language, the way she sat and the way her fingers hit the keys.

I asked mom if I could take piano lessons and she said "No, you can't." I asked, "Why not?" Her answer was, "Well, you can't hear, silly." But I thought I could do it. I was sure I could. I never thought, "I'm Deaf and can't play the piano." Nevertheless, my mother said I couldn't just because I couldn't hear. Her answer made no sense. I knew my fingers could do it!

My sister did teach me a few things on the piano. I memorized the notes. I didn't hear a thing so I can't say I enjoyed it but I did like plunking on the piano keys. Once my sister taught me some notes and I had fun playing them repeatedly. A few days later, one of my sister's friends heard me playing. Shocked, she asked, "How do you know how to play?" She was totally flabbergasted. I told her, "My sister taught me, that's all." Ha!

## My Brother Vinny

My brother Vinny was the baby in the family. I was four years old when he was born. I don't remember much about him.

When he and I talk about old times, he seems to remember a great deal more than I do. He'll say, "Don't you remember this? Don't you remember that? When we laughed? When we cried?" I don't have a clue what he's talking about. Maybe because he heard all this stuff and I didn't.

Pop tried to persuade Vinny to go to college but he never went. He was lucky and found a job at Grey Advertising agency as a mail boy. Later he moved up to become a TV Film Producer. Quite good for someone without a college degree!

Once, when Vinny was about ten and I was fourteen, we were fingerspelling in church to each other. I remember feeling surprised that he knew how and feeling thrilled that he could. Unfortunately he hardly knows it now because he doesn't use it often enough.

Vinny was always a special uncle to my sister's children and mine. He and his wife Nancy are my son Paul's Godparents. Vinny and Paul have similar interests: both love cooking traditional Italian foods. Maybe its part of our genes! When Paul was little, he looked up to Uncle Vinny and wanted to work in advertising, too. That didn't happen but they are still close.

### Vinny's New Kitchen Surprise

Once my brother invited us to his house for dinner. When we got there, we saw that he had just remodeled the entire kitchen: a new floor, cabinets, refrigerator, everything. His wife, Nancy, was showing me around the new, gorgeous kitchen. Vinny tapped me on the shoulder, saying, "Rose, Come with me. I'd like to show you something special." He pointed to a particular shelf and said, "Open this cabinet." When I opened the cabinet, I saw his TTY sitting on a sliding shelf. I almost cried. I didn't know what to say. Neither did my husband, Vincent. All we could do was stand there in shock.

He said proudly, "You know, Rose, you're a big part of my life. Nancy's always in the kitchen. I'm frequently there, too. We often call you from the kitchen and we wanted the call to be easy and convenient."

My brother impressed my friends. They didn't think any of their hearing family members would bother building a special shelf for a TTY just to call their Deaf relative.

### Vinny Surprises Me

About fifteen years ago, my brother's son got married. During the ceremony my brother, Vinny, made a speech. I remember watching him, not understanding. I didn't mind at all. Not understanding family events was "normal." After the ceremony he came over and gave me a copy of his speech. His sensitivity touched me. He knew I needed to be included. At the time, we never considered having an interpreter. What he did was perfect.

### Vinny Reminds Me to Get An Interpreter for Mom's Funeral

When my mother died, naturally I was upset and not thinking clearly. During the wake, I was exhausted and felt overwhelmed by people coming to pay their respects. At one point, Vinny came over and reminded me to make sure I had arranged an interpreter for the funeral service. He has become quite sensitive to my needs.

### How My Siblings and I Were Treated . . . Comparisons

I think mom and pop were very fair with the three of us. I would watch what they did and I look back now, as an adult, and I think they treated us fairly. They showed their support for me. For instance, mom always went if I had problems at school or the school had a meeting. She would willingly go to school and talk with any of our teachers. I think she treated us very much the same. Obviously I didn't see her go to my sister or brother's school, but when I needed her, she was there. I don't feel she treated me any differently because I was Deaf.

# CHAPTER 5.

## VINCENT

### Meeting Vincent as a Child, A Teenager and Again at 18

Vincent in his sanitation uniform, about 1948

I knew Vincent Pizzo when I was seven years old. I remember him clearly and can picture him. When I got on the school bus, Vincent was already on it, in the back with the older kids. We went to the same school for the deaf. Vincent still tells people he remembers me, in my pigtails, holding pop's hand, as he led me onto the school bus. One morning when I was about fourteen or fifteen years old, I was waiting for the school bus on Roosevelt Avenue. A garbage truck came by and parked right in front of where I was standing. Vincent jumped off the truck wearing a sanitation uniform with a cute little cap. He looked so handsome! He came over to me saying, "Hello. Remember me?" At that very moment, I think I fell in love with him. He was gorgeous and had the most magnificent smile. Of course, I said "Hello" back. I wasn't quite sure I remembered him, and replied, "I remember you a little bit. Did you sit in the back of the bus?" All I could remember was as a little kid, I always sat in the front of the bus, but the older kids sat in the back. He's seven years older so he would have been with the bigger kids. His face was familiar. After that accidental meeting, I didn't see him again for a few years. But honestly, I was in love with him. I'm sure of it. It happened that very day, but life went on and I went through my teenage years. I dated others and, like all teenagers, went to lots of parties.

**My First Date with Vincent**

When I was about 18 and Vincent was about 24, I was still living in Queens with my family. A group of friends and I went to Staten Island for Field Day. It was a major effort to get to Staten Island from Queens; it required a bus, train and the ferry! Our basketball team, the "Blue Swans," was playing against New Jersey and Staten Island teams.

Later in the evening, we went to a party at the clubhouse. Vincent was there. He looked like a gangster, dressed in a dark suit with a white tie. No kidding! He came over and again asked if I remembered him. This time I told him I did, so we chitchatted for a while. He started to flirt with me and we could both feel the electricity between us. At the end of the evening, he offered to drive me home from Staten Island all the way to Queens. Soon after that, he asked me to go out with him. That became our first date.

Believe it or not our first date was in New Jersey! It was 1950. Vincent picked me up at home and we met a group of friends at Palisades Amusement Park which had roller coasters and a huge swimming pool. We spent the day together and the rest is history! We started dating and went steady for about two years. My parents fell in love with Vincent the first time they met him. They knew he was the right guy for me. Maybe because he was Italian, or because his name was Vincent, the same as my brother's and my cousin who died so young. Or maybe just because he was terrific. Whatever the reason, Vincent was delighted, loved my parents and enjoyed their attention.

At the time I started dating Vincent, he was living with his older sister, Josephine. Vincent was youngest of eight children, the baby in his family. His mom died when he was thirteen; Josephine took care of the family throughout their mom's long illness. Then his father died of cancer when Vincent was about nineteen. Vincent always reminded me how close he had been to his father. Vincent was so proud when he learned to drive. He drove his dad all over Queens. One year before graduation, his father became extremely sick and Vincent had to leave school to support the family. He gave his entire salary to his dad. When we began dating, my parents became his "substitute parents" since both of his parents were gone.

### Vincent's Family

Vincent's family was very much like a "Deaf family." Of the eight children, six were hearing and two were Deaf, Vincent and one of his older sisters, Mamie. The four girls came first, then the four boys. Vincent was the youngest of the boys. The next youngest brother, Dominic, died in the second World War. I was touched when our son, Paul, and his wife, Linda, named their son after Dominic. It was their way of honoring his memory.

None of Vincent's siblings ever learned to sign, not even his Deaf sister, Mamie. His parents would not allow her to sign. Although she went to P.S. 47 and is profoundly Deaf, she barely learned to sign. After school, his family didn't allow her to socialize with Deaf people. They wanted her to grow up in the hearing world and didn't want her to have Deaf friends. She was a good lip reader, eventually married a hearing man and did end up living in the hearing world.

In my family everybody was hearing except me. They all talked and left me out. They didn't explain things to me and, if they did, because I asked questions, I got the abbreviated version. However, I noticed both Vincent and I could lipread everyone in his family. I think it's because they had two Deaf children (Vincent and Mamie) and two Deaf cousins. None of the hearing family members could sign but they knew how to move their lips so we could lipread them. They also used home signs and gestures. I remember thinking, "It's easy to communicate at Vincent's house, although almost everyone is hearing." Vincent's family members waved their hands to get someone's attention, then they started to talk. Deaf people do that all the time. His family just seemed naturally to understand cultural things about how to interact with Deaf people, although they did not sign.

For example, if I went to a wedding or a funeral with Vincent's family, I never felt left out. Never. It's not that his hearing relatives used sign language. However, they knew how to move their hands, use facial expressions and move their mouths in ways we could understand. In comparison, my family was more reserved than Vincent's. They rarely used facial expression and almost never gestured while they spoke.

**Vincent Proposes**

I expected Vincent to get on his hands and knees and ask me to marry him. It didn't happen. We started to talk about marriage one day and that was it. We decided we'd get engaged because we were one hundred percent sure of each other and we were happy together, so why not get married?

We had an engagement party with his family and my family. I thought we'd get engaged privately, just the two of us, alone. But his sister said, "Absolutely not." She insisted we get engaged, get the ring, at the party. I was absolutely furious, but what could I say? I couldn't tell him what to do, so he gave me the ring at the party, in public, with the families. It turned out nicer than I thought.

**Vincent—Previously Engaged**

There was somebody else who had been briefly engaged to Vincent. After he gave this other person a ring, he realized she was not the right woman for him. I don't know the exact details, but I do know it was short. He apparently said to her, "I've decided not to marry you." The poor girl was absolutely beside herself. She wanted him desperately but he didn't want her anymore. He didn't want to marry her and didn't want to be engaged to her.

One day, after they broke up, the girl's father came over to Vincent's house with a gun. He was, as you can imagine, a bad-tempered person. Vincent's brother-in-law, Tom, came out of the house to see what was going on and to try to calm the father down. The father did go away and didn't use the gun. Vincent never knew what the brother-in-law and the father said because it was between two hearing people. He never did learn the details. All he knew was he was not engaged and the father went away.

### My Wedding Gown

Vincent's Deaf sister, Mamie, made my gown and all of the gowns for the rest of the wedding party, the bridesmaids and family members. We're still friends with all of them today. Unfortunately, one of them, Kathleen, is in a nursing home now, suffering from Alzheimers.

Mamie did the sewing but I designed my gown, the bridesmaid's gowns, and made all the color and style decisions. Of course, the first thing was finding material. It felt like we went to a million places in New York but I couldn't find any fabrics I liked. Finally we went to Bonwit Teller, which, at the time, sold material although they haven't in a long time. I walked in and saw exactly what I wanted. It was more than I had imagined and ever dreamed about. However, it was $80.00 a yard. Can you imagine, $80 a yard in the 1950's? I didn't care. I wanted it. I wanted the best wedding in the world. Since my design had a huge pleated train, we had to find a place to make it. The pattern I designed was complicated and hard but Mamie was an expert dressmaker. The gowns were gorgeous and, after they pleated the train, Mamie made the rest of the gown.

**Our Wedding Day**

Rose and Vincent, our wedding, June 8, 1952

On the day of our wedding, the weather was absolutely gorgeous, a perfect "ten." The ceremony was at my childhood church, Saint Gabriel's, in East Elmhurst. Many of our neighbors came and enjoyed the magnificent roses blooming in the garden in front of my house. Of course, like all brides and grooms, it was the happiest day of our lives. I can't even remember where the reception was but I know we had a big wedding, about 200 people.

Some people have asked how Vincent and I understood the wedding ceremony since, in those days, we did not have an interpreter. This is what happened. The priest showed us the words in the book. We read them and said, "I do." That was it.

**Our Honeymoon**

When we left for our honeymoon, Vincent's family and my family were scared to death. They were worried about us because we were on our own for the first time. They were frantic something might happen to us though I was twenty and Vincent was twenty-seven. Picture this. They came with us to the airport to make sure we got on our flight to Florida. At least a million times, they asked, "Are you okay?" "Don't talk to strangers," they warned us. In contrast, Vincent and I were totally confident. We weren't afraid of anything. We flew to Florida, checked into the hotel, went swimming, and enjoyed the restaurants and tours. My sister had been married the year before and she had recommended the hotel. But we made all the arrangements. Although my sister called the hotel for us, I say, "We made the arrangements," because we made the decisions. Other people had to make the calls for us because there were no TTY's in those days.

One morning we went swimming at the beach and noticed another couple. They weren't on their honeymoon, but it was their first anniversary. The young woman was from France and the husband was American. They were sweet and struck up a conversation with us. Then they invited us to join them for dinner to celebrate our wedding and their first anniversary. We agreed and had a lovely evening together.

# CHAPTER 6.

## BECOMING PARENTS

**Nancy**

Nancy, our first child, was born in Paterson, in Barnert Hospital in 1956. We were still living in the Fair Lawn garden apartments.

Our hearing neighbors were lovely. We became friends with the family next door and the people above us. Mom made friends with them too, and somehow made sure they kept an eye on us. I thought it was a bit overprotective, but that's the way it was. When I was pregnant with Nancy, my mother and Vincent's family were very worried about us.

Back then, since there were no TTY's, we depended on others to make our phone calls. Our upstairs neighbor and I agreed on a warning signal. They said, "If you're ready, and you're in labor, send Vincent up to ring my bell three times and we'll use my phone to call the doctor." One night my labor pains started. However, Vincent rang the bell once instead of the agreed upon three rings. My neighbor knew, flew downstairs to make sure I was in labor, then called the doctor to tell him I would meet him at the hospital. We rushed to the hospital, but it was false labor. Doctor Krakower kept me in the hospital anyway, just for observation. Maybe because I had no way to contact him. He was wonderful. I loved him.

The doctor kept me overnight in the hospital and Nancy was finally born, in the late afternoon of the next day. I named her after Nancy Bloom, Ed Bloom's daughter. When Nancy Bloom was a child, she rode the school bus with me. She was an adorable, bright little girl. I always felt like I was baby sitting for her. Because of my relationship with Nancy Bloom, I always liked the name Nancy, so Vincent and I agreed to name our first child after her. Nancy's middle name is Grace, named for my mother, her grandma.

Many years later, I ran into Nancy Bloom, who is Nancy Raurus now. She knew I named Nancy after her. Her middle name is Grace but I hadn't known it. I had not only used Nancy's first name but somehow had selected her middle name, too! Wow! Imagine that!

We christened Nancy at St. Gabriel's in East Elmhurst. Her Godparents are my sister Frances and her husband Jerry.

### The Chase With Nancy's Baby Formula

My mother wanted me to come to East Elmhurst after Nancy was born so she could help take care of us. We agreed I would stay for two weeks. This was back in the days of baby formulas. After the two weeks, Vincent and I left with Nancy to return to Fair Lawn but mom realized we had left the formula in Queens. As we were on the road coming back to Fair Lawn, my brother-in-law, Jerry, was trying to catch up with us. Shortly after we got home with Nancy, Jerry rang the doorbell saying, "You left the formula in Queens. Here it is." I was embarrassed, but I was a new mother and you just have to expect things like that.

### Karen

In 1958 when Karen was born, we were still living in the same three room garden apartments. TTY's were still not available. Our upstairs neighbors had moved but I had made more friends in the neighborhood. My labor pains started in the afternoon. Soon, there were seven neighbors in my apartment. They kept asking me, "Are you okay? Are you okay?" They debated who would call the doctor and how to take care of me. They timed my contractions. I remember a neighbor saying, "She doesn't seem ready. Her contractions don't seem strong enough."

That was my way. I was too embarrassed to show my labor pains were sharp and hurt plenty. I remember they filled my living room, watching every move I made. Karen, like Nancy, was born in Barnert Hospital. Again Dr. Krakauer was the Ob-Gyn.

Karen's christening was at Saint Catherine's Church in Glen Rock because that was the church for our parish. Her godparents were Vincent's brother Joe, and his wife, Helen.

**Paul**

When Paul was born, in 1962, we had just moved to the house on Remington Road. The sweet little house was the perfect size for our growing family. I knew when my labor pains started, I would have to leave the girls home. Before I left for the hospital, I decided they needed a bath. I was doubled over with labor pains, crying because I didn't want to leave the girls. I gave them a bath, put them in their pajamas, and made sure they were neat and clean.

Again, my mother worried about me. There were still no TTY's but we had arranged for a neighbor, Helen, to come over when I went into labor. Helen would watch the kids and take care of calling the doctor. When Vincent went to tell her I was in labor, she was in the middle of brushing her teeth. She rushed in, with her toothbrush in her mouth, trying to talk to me. I couldn't understand a thing she said because she had this toothbrush sticking out of her mouth! We finally understood she planned to go to a banquet with her husband that night.

She called my Deaf friend, Rose, to come over. Rose's nine year old hearing son answered the phone. He told his mom we needed her to come over and watch Karen and Nancy so Vincent could take me to the hospital. Rose said, "Rose will have to wait. I have to finish my dishes and then I'll come over." Can you picture this? I'm in labor and she's finishing her dishes! Ha! Then my neighbor, Helen, called my mom in Jackson Heights. Naturally, mom dropped everything and came out to Fair Lawn by train and bus. It was a long time ago. Imagine having to depend on neighbors to make phone calls! Today it's simple. We use the

TTY or relay to contact one another and then we just get in the car and go.

### Deaf Parenting

When I got married, I learned how to become an independent person, especially after I moved to New Jersey. I was kind of scared to face a new life in New Jersey and, of course, I made many mistakes. I was young. I was Deaf and I didn't know how to do many things on my own. While I was growing up, mom took care of phone calls and my sister took care of a million other things for me.

When Nancy was born, Vincent and I went straight from the hospital to East Elmhurst to stay with my mom and the family. They were very concerned about Vincent and me becoming parents. They thought I couldn't take care of a baby because I couldn't hear. The whole family was watching me because they didn't quite trust me to know what to do. Was it because I was Deaf or because we were new parents? Maybe both. When Nancy cried, they didn't tell me because they were afraid I'd spoil her!

Many people asked me, "How did you hear the baby cry?" or "How did you know if the baby was upset?" I told them we had a special baby cry device, a microphone attached to the crib. In the daytime, if Nancy cried, the microphone picked up the baby's voice and caused lights to flash throughout the house. At night, if she cried, the microphone was hooked up to a device that caused our bed to vibrate. We definitely felt safe with those two devices. Like many new moms, I would wake up in the middle of the night, take a quick peek and make sure she was okay. I was always afraid she would stop breathing or get smothered in a blanket.

Being a parent was a scary experience for me. I just didn't know anything. It was harder being a Deaf parent than a hearing parent. I felt afraid something would happen to them. For instance, when I was living in the apartment before we moved to the house on Remington, we had only one bedroom. Nancy and Karen slept in our bedroom: Nancy in the crib and Karen in the basinet. Having them with me was just easier for me because I could watch them both. I would wake up in the middle of the night, look at them and go back to sleep.

When Paul was born and we were living on Remington Road, he, too, slept in our room. He slept there until he was almost three years old. I just felt more secure having him with us to keep an eye on him at night.

I had a Deaf friend who was older than I. She was surprised to see my vibrating baby crier. She told me when her children were babies, each night when she went to bed, she tied a string from their toes to her arm. If the baby cried, she would feel the string pulling on her. That impressed me. I thought it was a creative and clever idea. Deaf people usually figure out smart ways to make up for things they can't hear.

HOLIDAY

GREETINGS

from our
house
to yours

The Pizzo's
Vincent, Rose, Nancy, Karen & Paul

Holiday card 1964

## Paul Knows We Are Deaf

When Paul was about two or three years old, he would wake up early every morning. He was a quiet toddler. He wouldn't call me. He wouldn't cry but he was awake. The house only had two bedrooms since this was before Vincent finished the upstairs rooms. Paul's crib was in our room and the two older girls slept in the other bedroom. Paul somehow figured out if he threw his stuffed animals at me, I would wake up. After that, I made sure he had stuffed animals in his bed to throw!

When Paul was about two and a half years old, he was taking a nap while I was down in the basement doing the laundry. At the time, we had a dog, Rusty. I noticed Rusty frantically running up and down the stairs. Something felt wrong. After I flew up the stairs, I saw Paul, in his crib, crying and screaming hysterically. I didn't know he was crying because we didn't have the microphone hooked up to the lights in the basement! There sat Paul, with the microphone tangled around and squeezing his finger. I thought my heart would break seeing this toddler clinging to the microphone trying to call me, not knowing I couldn't hear his cries for help. Somehow the dog knew to alert me! What would have happened without Rusty?

Another time Paul and I were on our way home from the pool. One of his favorite friends was a neighbor, who lived two doors away from us. She was an old woman who adored Paul. We called her "Nana." On the way home from the pool Paul wanted to stop and say "hello" to Nana but I told him he couldn't. He pleaded with me all the way home. Nana's daughter saw us arguing outside. She came over and I explained the reason we were arguing and she said, "This is a perfect time to see Nana." She brought us over to the old screened porch: me, Paul, Nana, and her daughter, Edna. I couldn't understand Nana's speech. I couldn't lipread her but Paul was interpreting! He wasn't quite signing, but he was oral interpreting what she was saying. Paul was only about four or five years old. Nana talked to Paul, and Paul turned to me saying, "Nana said, . . . " and he repeated everything she said. The conversation went on like that for a long time. Paul throughly impressed me, and Nana too. That's probably why their relationship was so terrific.

Once Vincent had an accident at work. While he was closing the garage door, he hit his chin and began bleeding profusely. They took him to the hospital, where the doctor stitched his chin. Because it was a work-related accident, he had to go to the Labor Board. Paul was only two years old but we took him with us to the courtroom. The courts did not have interpreters in those days. The three of us sat way in the back of the courtroom, with Paul on my lap. We had no idea what was happening. We didn't think to tell the court clerk we were Deaf and just sat in the back. I wrote a note to the man next to me asking him to tell me if he heard our name, "Pizzo." When they called our name, "Vincent Pizzo," little Paul smacked my face. What an incredible thing for a two year old to do! He was an impressive, sensitive child. That's how we knew they were calling us. He knew, at an early age we were Deaf, and he knew ways to make sure our needs were met.

### Teaching Honesty

Once Paul went to the bank to cash a check. When he got home, he counted the money and noticed he had ten dollars too much. I told him, "Don't worry about it. Keep it." He turned around, went back to the bank and returned the ten dollars. Firmly, he said, "I could not possibly keep the money." I felt guilty afterwards. I knew I had done the wrong thing, but he knew what was right! Soon after, Vincent and I cashed a check and the clerk gave us $200 too much. I remembered Paul's experience and immediately took the money back to the bank. No way I was going to keep the $200!

### Saint Anne's School

Vincent and I sent the three children to Saint Anne's school beginning with the first grade. We wanted them to learn about their religion. Vincent and I never learned much about our Catholic religion because we were Deaf and never had the opportunity to go to CCD like the hearing kids. All of the children received communion and their confirmation at Saint Anne's. During the ceremonies, I never understood what was going on. I was ignorant. I understood they received communion and I understood they received the wafer but I didn't understand much more. These were the days before interpreters!

The children's school had parent meetings. Although I always went to them, I never understood what was going on. I never realized I was supposed to know many things. I was used to not understanding many things. When the meetings were over, I would go over to the teacher and explain that I was Deaf. They never seemed interested or helpful. I would just ask the teacher how Karen, Nancy or Paul were doing and I'd get a brief answer, usually something like, "Everything is fine." Then I would leave. I know the other parents got more and watched them talking with the teachers for a long time. I saw them ask questions and get long answers. That never happened to me.

### Karen's Friends and Me

When Karen was a student at Saint Anne's, she was extremely shy. I'm sure she was embarrassed because Vincent and I were Deaf, but she was also nervous or afraid of people. When she started school, everything seemed fine, but she didn't invite her friends to the house. She always went to their houses. I would tell her, "Come on. You know, you can invite your friends to the house. It's good that you go to their houses but you should bring them here." One day I went to pick up Karen from school, but she didn't know I was coming. I parked the car and I saw all the kids playing in the yard. Karen and I made eye contact. I looked at her face and I knew she was embarrassed. Then I understood. Of course, she came up to me. When they saw me in the car, all of her friends came rushing over to me and said, "Hi Mrs. Pizzo," with big smiles on their faces. Her friends knew I was Deaf but they had never communicated with me. Karen then introduced me to all her friends. "This is Dot and this is Pat. This is so-and-so," and they all seemed thrilled to say "hello" to me. They seemed friendly.

From that moment on, Karen invited her friends to the house. I guess that broke through Karen's embarrassment. After that, Karen seemed proud to introduce me to her friends. She would say, "My mother and father are Deaf. This is my mom and dad." Those kids have become so close to me, sometimes I call them "my daughters" because they spent so much time here. They were very comfortable in our house. They could talk with me, and they still are comfortable around me.

Just recently Karen just bought a house across the street. It's a Cape Cod house, just like ours. I almost feel like I can watch my house get born again as she begins to fix hers up.

**After High School**

After Nancy graduated from high school, she didn't want to go to college. Her piano teacher encouraged her to study music but we felt it would be too expensive. During high school Nancy had been involved in a work-study program at Liberty Insurance Company. Instead of going to college or music school she decided to stay with Liberty Mutual and she's been there ever since. Soon, it'll be 25 years! Karen decided she wanted to be a secretary and went to Katherine Gibbs School. Both Karen and Nancy have done well, working independently, on their own.

Paul couldn't decide what he wanted to do when he graduated from high school. He started working at a variety of part time jobs. For a while, he worked at Bob Lapsley's machine shop. Bob was one of our neighbors. Soon after, he decided he wanted to do copy machine repair. Now he works for the telephone company in Chicago, Illinois.

**The Second Nellie**

When Paul was around eighteen, he was working in my neighbor's machine shop. A stray dog walked into the machine shop and sat next to Paul. This poor dog was just a mess. Somebody had sprayed paint all over him and his fur was matted with chewing gum. Paul asked his boss if he could put him in the corner, give him water and a little bit of food. Of course, after that, the dog fell in love with Paul and, at the end of the day, Paul wanted to keep the dog. He knew he couldn't just leave it at work!

Paul brought the dog home. He warned me, "Mom, I brought this lost dog home and want to keep him." I said "Paul, no way. There's not a chance in the world you can keep this dog here." Paul begged and pleaded, "Please let me give him a bath. Let me feed him. I can't just get rid of him." I finally relented, and figured, "Okay. He'll bathe him and I'll let him stay one day." Of course, the next day Paul begged me again. I felt so sorry for this poor dog, I agreed. I told Paul, "You can keep the dog on one condition. You have to name this dog Nellie." We kept Nellie in our family for fourteen years.

### Using the Children to Make Phone Calls for Us

Back when Nancy was born, we didn't have a TTY. If we needed to make a phone call, we would ask a neighbor. At some point, when Nancy was five or six years old, I felt she was old enough to make calls for us. Poor Nancy. She hated it but we needed her to do it and she did. When Karen was old enough, she learned how and they took turns. Paul learned how, too, but most of the time we depended on Nancy because she was the oldest.

### Santa

When our children were little, I can't remember who played Santa Claus. Sometimes one of my cousin's husband and sometimes pop. Of course, Vincent was never Santa Claus. Never. The children would have known right away it was their dad because he couldn't talk to them. We didn't want them to know their daddy was Santa Claus.

### Karen's Cheerleading . . . Paul Gives Us His Perspective

Karen was a cheerleader at Saint Anne's. She and her friends took their cheerleading seriously, and practiced constantly. Naturally, like other moms, I car pooled to cheerleading practice and the games. Paul often came along.

One year when Paul was about eight, Karen's cheerleading squad competed in a tournament. When Vincent, Paul and I got there, we saw the place was packed with parents, relatives and friends. Vincent and I, of course, couldn't understand the cheers, but we enjoyed watching. We wanted to be there to support Karen and her team. Each time a cheerleading team finished, little Paul tapped us on the shoulder and asked if we liked them. We didn't know what to say because we couldn't hear their cheers. Paul gave us his opinion each time. He said, "They're just so-so." or "They're not terrific," or "This group is good." When Karen's team finished, Paul tapped us and pointed saying, "They are the best." Honestly, to me, the kids shaking pom poms all looked the same. I couldn't tell one group from the next. Paul insisted, "Mom, you should hear Karen's group. They are absolutely the best." I thought to myself, "Naturally, Paul thinks Karen's group is the best. He wants his sister to win." However, eight-year-old Paul was right. Karen's team won first place in New Jersey.

Paul knew we couldn't hear the cheers but he figured out how to include us in the event. He didn't "interpret the cheers," but gave us his opinion. Many children of Deaf parents, called coda (child of Deaf adult) do things like that.

### My Best Friend Louise

Louise was my best friend at P.S. 47 from the time we met in second grade. In school we were always together. We hung out together at lunch, in the halls and in the playground. She lived in the Bronx and I lived in Queens. As soon as we were old enough to take the bus alone, we saw each other on weekends. Most of the time she came to my house because she adored my big family. My house was a busy place compared to hers. At my house, my brother, sister, cousins, aunts and uncles were always coming and going.

Often we did what girls like to do: we traded clothes. We would try on each other's clothes and then switch outfits. I have a whole pile of pictures of me in her clothes and her in mine. If one of us needed to go out, we would always give the other something lovely to wear.

Louise's parents were hearing, and like my family, they didn't sign. Everything at her house was oral. Her parents and mine became good friends. I think Louise and I needed each other. Like all close friends, we shared our problems and frustrations about home and school. We had "girl-talk" where we gossiped about clothes, boys and school.

Louise adored being around my large family, with my brother, sister and cousins. She was an only child until she was a teenager. When she was about fourteen, she nagged her mother, "Please let me have brothers and sisters. Have another baby because I want a sister and brother like Rose." Sure enough, her mother became pregnant. Can you imagine? She had twin girls, both hearing. Louise came to school one day and said, "My mom had two babies." She never said "twins." Then, maybe we didn't even know the word "twins." Everybody at school was stunned. Louise was happy and excited about her twin sisters. Once, Louise asked me to help her with the twins and I did. We both felt quite grown up that her mom trusted us with them. One twin is still in touch with me and sends me a Christmas card every year.

Louise and I met when we started school at P.S. 47. We were both seven years old, a little late to start school. We stayed close friends all through our school days. Though I went to a hearing high school and she went directly to work, our friendship continued. When we were teenagers, we double dated. As young married couples, we took vacations together. Our children were born at around the same time. Her two children, Lorraine and Linda, were both Deaf. Louise was upset that her children were Deaf. I agreed with her back then. But now I think it was a gift for her to have Deaf children. In my family, Vincent and I understood our children when they spoke to us. They learned, from the time they were toddlers, to look at us and to pronounce words clearly. But to be honest, if they talked only to each other, Vincent and I were lost. Louise's family didn't have that communication problem. They all were Deaf and they all signed. Communication was simple and accessible to all of them.

Our families got together often. Although her children were Deaf and mine were hearing, they got along beautifully. Her children would try to lipread mine. Mine did not sign very much but they gestured and spoke. My children understood her children's speech, gestures and signs.

Louise and I were so close. I was the godmother of her second child, Linda. I am still in touch with Linda. She's married to a wonderful man, Bill, and has two beautiful children. The boy is Deaf and the daughter is hearing. Of course, the daughter signs fluently since she has Deaf parents, grandpa Bill and Aunt Lorraine, as well as Deaf friends.

Louise died tragically, in the early 70's, just about the time that Linda was just going to be "Sweet Sixteen." I had lost touch with Louise a few years before that. One day, her mother-in-law called me to tell me the bad news. We didn't have a TTY then, so when she called she reached Paul who was eight or nine year's old. She asked Paul to get paper and pencil and told him to write a note to me. She told him to write, "Louise died." Paul wrote exactly as she said. When I got home Paul said "I have a note for you, mom." When I looked at the note I was dumbfounded. She was my best friend and I didn't even know she had been ill. All I could do was bawl.

There were gas shortages in the early 70's. People were only allowed to buy gas on odd or even numbered days, depending on how their license plate ended. Louise's wake and funeral were in Pearl River and I wasn't sure we had enough gas for both trips. But I knew that I had to go. Somehow we managed to get enough gas. I sobbed until I thought my heart would break. I couldn't stop crying and hugging the children. Vincent and I stayed close with Bill and the children after that. Bill recently died. Even now, I get a Mother's Day card from my godchild, Linda, and I still feel connected with her. Vincent and I visit her from time to time.

Both of Louise's daughters work at the Maryland School for the Deaf. Linda is the Dean of Students and her sister, Lorraine, teaches art, art history and photography. Jason, Linda and Bill's Deaf son, is a student there, too. Linda and Bill have a hearing daughter, Lydia, who is a coda (child of deaf adults). When Lydia was a child, she wanted to go to the Maryland School for the Deaf, too. She was disappointed when Linda told her she couldn't because she was hearing. In fact, one day Lydia joined the school's cheerleading squad, and was able to follow all the cheers in sign. Like most codas, ASL is her native language and she saw no reason not to join the fun.

# CHAPTER 7.

## WE MOVE TO NEW JERSEY

### Why We Moved to Fair Lawn

When Vincent and I got married, I was working in Manhattan. For the first two years of our marriage, we lived with my parents in Queens. We were trying to save money to buy furniture. Vincent also worked in Manhattan but he wasn't earning much. A Deaf friend from New Jersey, Richard Meyers, had an uncle who owned a company, Einson Freeman, in Fair Lawn, NJ. Richard recommended Vincent for a die cutting position and Vincent began to work for them. The commute was an hour each way. After a while, he was exhausted just from the commuting, especially in the winter. He suggested we move to Fair Lawn. It sounded like a good idea to me. I didn't see any reason to continue staying with my parents.

Both of our families were quite upset about our decision to move to New Jersey. They were worried and concerned about our living "on our own." I wasn't. I felt totally confident I could handle anything. Besides, East Elmhurst wasn't very far away, only forty five minutes. We found a garden apartment in Fair Lawn for $75 a month. We had terrific neighbors. After my parents met them, they were satisfied. Mom knew the neighbors were "looking out for us."

Vincent worked for Einson Freeman for about twenty years. Eventually, the business began to slow and Vincent was only working four days a week. Fortunately, another Deaf friend of

Vincent's knew about a job opening in New York at Reliable Press. He worked for them for almost eighteen years and put up with the long commute. It was well worth it. The money was much better, had good benefits, and he had a good future.

**Vincent's Hearing Sister Thinks We Can't Take Care of Ourselves**

When Vincent and I moved to New Jersey, Vincent's sister, Josephine, thought there was no way we could live by ourselves because we were deaf. She worried because we couldn't hear the doorbell and we didn't have a phone. She was hysterical. "Your parents have to live with you. They need to take care of you," she kept telling us. The two deaf cousins in their family lived with their parents so she thought we had to live with my parents. I remember saying to her, "No way. We can do our own thing. We can take care of ourselves."

As the years went by, she saw us raise our three children. I worked hard to teach them proper manners. Once we visited Josephine on Mother's Day. Each child brought her a bouquet of flowers and wished her a "Happy Mother's Day." They impressed Josephine. That day, she admitted she didn't think we would make it. She admired our lovely children and told us how beautifully Vincent and I were raising them. She was thrilled we were independent and was glad she had been wrong.

I can't blame her for her feelings. They were based on her experience. She took care of her two deaf siblings, Vincent and Mamie, after their mother died. Fortunately, Vincent knew he didn't need anyone to take care of him.

Before Vincent met me, his family wanted him to marry a hearing woman. They fixed him up with different hearing women. When Vincent was dating me, a Deaf woman, they were not thrilled at all. They told him bluntly they were not happy he was dating somebody Deaf. But we got engaged and then married and the rest is history.

Vincent's sister, Mamie, did marry a hearing man and lived in the hearing world. Josephine controlled Mamie's life. In fact,

Mamie and her hearing husband and son even lived with Josephine and her family!

## My Fair Lawn Neighbors

When Vincent and I first moved to New Jersey from Queens, we lived in an apartment on Chandler Drive. At the time, we didn't have any children. I became extremely close friends with one of my neighbors, Phillis Lane. We had our first babies at around the same time and our life styles were very similar. Our friendship developed as we raised our children. She was quite an observant lady. For example, she noticed me watching television and asked me how I understood the programs. She asked me how I survived without a telephone. She seemed to understand the Deaf world was different from the hearing world. In those days, they did not caption TV programs, TTY's did not exist, and we had no telephone relay services.

The way Vincent and I managed our lives, impressed her. Phyllis lived above us in the garden apartments. One day her husband said to her, "You know Vincent and Rose never fight. I never hear them arguing with each other." Phyllis came to me and asked, "Don't you and Vincent fight? Don't you and Vincent argue? I've never heard you screaming and arguing?" "Of course we argue," I said, "but we do it in sign." Poor Phyllis, her mouth hit the floor. She never thought of that. It never occurred to her that we could argue in sign language. She and her husband learned a great deal about Deaf culture and the Deaf world from Vincent and me.

She always thought Vincent and I knew how to do things better. In some ways, they thought Vincent and I were perfect and did things perfectly. Of course, we weren't, but that was her impression of us. For example, when we bought a high chair for Nancy, they bought one for their son Jeffrey. When they looked at ours, they knew ours was better than theirs. Theirs was just kind of "so-so." Sometimes I would buy something for the kids and she would say, "Gosh you have such incredible taste. I wish I had your taste and knew how to buy things like you do."

We're still friends. We see each other less now, but we're still good friends. Her husband, who was a lawyer, died of cancer and she stayed in Fair Lawn for a while. She then moved to an apartment in Fort Lee, but we stay in touch. Our kids, who grew up together, are still very close friends. Nancy and Phyllis' son are the same ages. Karen and her daughter, Tracey, are about the same age and are still close.

### The House in Fair Lawn on Remington Road

After Nancy and Karen were born, the four of us were crowded in a one bedroom apartment on Chandler Drive. We began looking for a house, but we didn't want to leave Fair Lawn. Vincent looked in the newspaper, saw a house for sale in Fair Lawn and said, "Come on, let's look." We drove by this house and it looked like a lovely street but the house was an eyesore. It was overgrown with trees and looked neglected. Vincent said, "Let's just go see. We don't have to go in the house. Let's just look." As we pulled up to the house, he must have felt my resistance. He tried to calm me down, saying, "Don't worry. I will fix it. I will paint it." Before we even walked in the house, he told me all these things. So we bought this house. Sure enough, what he said came true. At first, I wasn't happy because the house was so much work. But after a while, I began to love this house. We're still in it after almost 40 years.

When we got ready to move, we had to stay with my mom for two weeks. We could not just move into this house. Vincent needed pop to help him do the work. Pop never had a vacation in his entire life. He was a workaholic. He worked hard from the day he arrived in America. When Vincent and I bought the house on Remington Road, pop was in his late fifties. To help Vincent do all the things that needed to be done in the house, he took two weeks off from the shop. After those two weeks, he never again took another vacation. When my mom went to Italy, he didn't even go with her. Sad when you think about it.

On pop's only "vacation" in his life, the very first thing they did was paint the bedrooms because we needed a clean place to sleep! Then they remodeled the kitchen. They ripped out all the old cabinets. They ripped out everything—the refrigerator, the stove and the floor. You name it. It went. They broke down the wall and doorway that separated a tiny dinette from the kitchen. Then the kitchen/dinette became one big long room. They put in all new cabinets, a new refrigerator, new stove, everything new and shiny. Was I relieved! It was clean and beautiful.

And the living room! You wouldn't believe what was in the living room. The living room had at least fifty layers of wallpaper. They ripped all of it out. Vincent had to rent a machine to skim off the layers of wallpaper. The weather was brutally hot, so poor dad and Vincent were soaked with sweat. After they stripped off all the layers of wallpaper, they painted the living room. Then they painted all the rooms in the house: the two bedrooms, the living room, kitchenette, dining area and the bathroom. The upstairs wasn't finished at the time. It was just an attic. We didn't have the family room then either. The house only had two bedrooms. The two kids shared one bedroom and Vincent and I had the other.

About five years later, when I got pregnant with Paul, we felt we needed more space. We decided to add two more bedrooms upstairs and a family room next to the kitchen. Then the house would have room for our many friends and relatives. We didn't have any idea how to get town approval for an addition. The children were too young to call Borough Hall for us. Fortunately, my friend Phyllis was a tremendous help. She knew how to contact Borough Hall to get the various variances and permits we needed. She did all of it for us. Thank goodness for friends like Phyllis! We hired a carpenter to do the upstairs bathroom, the family room and the bedrooms. Vincent did the wallpapering and the paneling. Naturally, we had some help from family members and friends. For example, our nephew Sonny did the fireplace. Our Deaf friend, Bob Sabo, did the cabinets. Bob is the best carpenter you'd ever want to meet.

### The Radburn Association

When I first moved to the house on Remington Road, all I could see was how much repair the house needed. However my friend, Phyllis, said to me, "Do you realize how lucky you are to live in Radburn?" She knew the Radburn area was special, particularly for the children, but I didn't even know what she was talking about. I had never heard of the Radburn Association. I found out the Association provided a variety of recreational activities: a pool, archery programs, programs for toddlers, swimming lessons and tennis and a whole variety of summer programs. When people bought houses in Radburn, they had to join the Radburn Association.

When the original owners bought this house, they did not want to join the Radburn Association and because of that, my house was not part of it. They would not allow my children to participate in Radburn Association activities. Fortunately, Phyllis' husband, Jerry, was a lawyer. He helped us write a letter to the Association asking the Board to let us join. His letter explained we were a Deaf couple, with hearing children. He said our children needed to join the Association's recreational programs so they would not be isolated. My own childhood experiences, feeling left out, made me aware of how important it was for my children to play with neighborhood children. I was desperate to keep the children from having the same experience and was grateful for Jerry's help with the letter to the Board. Fortunately, they accepted Jerry's reasoning and let us become members.

The house on the corner of Remington Road and Berdan Avenue also wanted to join the Radburn Association. After we were successful, they tried again to get in but the Association turned them down. Eventually the family sold the house and bought another house in Radburn because they wanted to become part of the Association. Even today, that house on the corner is still not a member of the Association.

Maybe other issues were involved. All of the houses in this area, including ours, were built in the 1940's except two: one on the corner across the street and the house on the south side of us. Both were built many years later. Our house was never in the Association because of the decision of the original owners who didn't want to participate. I think the reason we were successful in being admitted was that our house was originally part of the Radburn development, while the other two were not.

They moved the house on the corner, on the south side of our house, from Fair Lawn Avenue to Remington and Berdan. The house across the street, on the corner, was also a new house, built way after they built the original Radburn houses. I think that is why those houses were never part of the Radburn Association. I also thought Jerry's letter about our being Deaf, made a difference in our being admitted too. I'll never know the real reason. I'm just glad we could join and the children could benefit from their wonderful recreational activities.

**Special Parties at Home in the Back Yard**

Vincent and I will soon celebrate our 47th anniversary. Our 25th anniversary was almost 25 years ago, but I want you all to know about our 25th anniversary party in the backyard. The whole family came. My sister and her family came from California, all our Deaf friends and hearing relatives came and filled the backyard. All our cousins, aunts and uncles came. We didn't cook for such a large crowd. Instead our children ordered food from a local caterer and we rented tables and chairs. Naturally I didn't hear the music, but I know we had it. When we had huge parties like these, we always had them catered and my wonderful children handled all the ordering.

**Mom and Pop Retire to Fair Lawn**

We were the only ones in the family to move to New Jersey. Everybody else stayed in Queens. Pop always said, during those years, "If I have to move, I am going to move near you and Vincent." He never said it was because I was Deaf. He said it because he felt close to Vincent and me. I think it was because he loved us so much.

Eventually pop retired. Shortly after, he came to visit when I had surgery to remove a thyroid tumor. Mom told me she and pop had decided to move to New Jersey. She said, "You know I always dreamed of moving into a little red house." Sure enough, they were driving around and mom said, "That's the house I want. That little red house." It was the cutest little house. It was a small red house on top of a hill just a couple of blocks away from our house, with a "For Sale" sign in front. They called the real estate agency and mom and pop bought that house. It was the first and only house they saw. The house was red, three blocks away and perfect.

It's interesting that they chose to live near us. They didn't want to live near my brother in Long Island or my sister in California. It's not that they came to live in Fair Lawn to help me raise my children. The kids were teenagers by the time they moved here. I had already raised my family without mom and pop looking over my shoulder. Looking back, I'm glad they stayed in Queens, until the children were almost grown. I would never have learned how to manage if they had been nearby. If we had stayed in Queens, they would have definitely controlled us. Our move to New Jersey was one of the best things Vincent and I ever did. We raised our children ourselves and developed independent, separate lives.

# CHAPTER 8.

## THE FAMILY GROWS

### Paul Meets Linda

Linda grew up in Illinois. She worked for Bellcore in Chicago and was transferred to New Jersey for two years. During that time, Karen was also working for Bellcore and she and Linda became friends. Karen decided to have a "black and white" party. She decorated everything in her apartment in black and white: balloons, paper tablecloths, paper plates, plastic silverware and all the party decorations. Karen invited Paul to the party, along with the young woman he was dating, and many friends. I think about 200 people were invited! Fortunately Karen shared an enormous apartment with a roommate. When Karen introduced Linda to Paul, it was love at first sight. At the end of the evening, Paul took his date home and went back to Karen's house because he was so attracted to Linda. Soon after, they started seeing each other and that was it. They were in love.

### Paul Tells Linda His Parents are Deaf

Linda was living in Hillsborough, New Jersey, a town about forty-five minutes from Fair Lawn. Paul wanted Linda to meet us, but he had not told her we were Deaf. I don't know if he kept it from her on purpose or just never bothered telling her because he thought it was normal. I clearly remember the night. Vincent and I were sitting at the kitchen table waiting for them to arrive. When she and Paul walked into the living room, Paul said, "By the way, my parents are Deaf." She was shocked and terrified to meet us. They stayed in the living room for almost half an hour talking about what to do. Vincent and I waited while Paul went to answer the door to let Linda in, but we waited and waited. Linda was stiff as a board. She shook our hands and said, "Pleased to meet you." It took a while until she warmed up. Communication was hard. We communicated through Paul but poor Linda was scared to death.

### Linda and Paul Become Engaged and Married

Linda's two years in New Jersey were ending and she knew she had to return to Bellcore in Chicago. However, she and Paul were becoming serious. Linda called her boss in Chicago and asked to stay in New Jersey. Fortunately he agreed. The night Paul gave Linda an engagement ring, they hurried home to show us.

Linda made plans with her mom for the wedding in Illinois. She listed things she needed to do. I can't believe how sensitive she was toward Vincent and me. The first thing on her list was hiring an interpreter. She asked her father to take care of it. Then she began to look for a gown and all the other necessary tasks for a wedding. I was impressed with her thinking of the interpreter as "Number One."

Sadly, soon after their engagement, they diagnosed Linda's mother with cancer and she began chemotherapy treatments. The treatments made her weak. In spite of her illness, her mom and dad wanted to come to New Jersey to meet Paul's family. They also wanted to see the small house Linda and Paul had bought. The doctor told Linda's mother she was too sick to travel but she ignored his advice. She insisted on coming to New Jersey. When her parents arrived, Linda realized how sick her mom was. Her father practically carried her mom off the plane. They came back to our house for dinner but her mom could not eat much. However, having the two families together was lovely.

Linda had told her parents Vincent and I were Deaf. When we met, to be honest, communication was hard. Both Linda and Paul worked at helping us communicate that evening. Her parents had never met a Deaf person, but when we were introduced, they were warm and happy to meet us. We felt comfortable with them and, gradually, as the evening progressed, communication improved. They were thrilled to be in New Jersey, meeting us and Paul's two sisters.

Two weeks later, after they returned to Chicago, her mom died. I was upset and shocked. I couldn't believe they made the trip, only two weeks before she died, just to meet us. Nevertheless, it happened. They got here on July 23, their anniversary, and she died August 7.

Planning the wedding for October 15, only two months later, was hard for Linda. Nevertheless, the wedding was beautiful, though we all missed Linda's mom. We had a whole block of rooms at the hotel in Chicago. Linda made lovely little baskets of food, candy and nuts for each room, a sweet and adorable welcome for out of town guests. My neighbors from Fair Lawn, the Lapsley's, came with their two sons, Johnny and Robby. The boys, close friends of Paul, were ushers in the wedding party. This time, the opposite of our own wedding, Vincent and I understood the entire ceremony, because we had an interpreter. Having that interpreter was fabulous. I felt comfortable because Linda and her family were accepting of us and recognized our needs.

### Linda Learns to Sign

As time went on, while Linda and Paul lived in New Jersey, Linda started paying more attention to how Vincent and I communicated. She began to ask us about various signs. After a while she said, "You know, I'd like to become an interpreter." When they moved back to Chicago, she enrolled in the Interpreter Training Program at Harper College. She had some hearing teachers and some Deaf teachers but she seemed to learn faster from the Deaf teachers. She was only able to stay in the program for two years. Sadly, her brother, Dan, became a widower when his wife, Anne, died suddenly. Dan was left with five young children, the youngest only two months old. Linda and Paul bought a house nearby and moved so Linda could help take care of them. Linda learned so much at Harper that we communicate smoothly! Every time the family is together, Linda acts as the interpreter. I love having a daughter-in-law, who can sign well and is willing to interpret too.

One afternoon, the three of us, Vincent, Linda and me, were practicing signs in the family room. Linda could hear conversations in the kitchen. She asked me, "You want to know what they're saying?" I said, "Sure." She started interpreting what everybody in the kitchen was saying. It was neat to be able to eavesdrop on a "hearing" conversation. We have a close relationship now and have become friends. Every time I go to Chicago, we go shopping together. We decorate the house together. Paul doesn't sign nearly as well as Linda. He pronounces every word carefully and fingerspells while he speaks but he doesn't use ASL. He's missing the ASL facial expression that is so important. Interestingly enough, every time I teach the children some signs, he learns them from the children. He wants me to teach the grandchildren ASL.

### Michelle, Our First Grandchild

Once when Linda and Paul came to visit from Chicago, they gave us a "Winnie the Pooh" book. I couldn't imagine why. It was their way of letting me know Linda was pregnant! Naturally, we were excited about our first grandchild.

When the baby arrived, they couldn't choose a name, but finally agreed on Michelle Rose. Vincent and I went out to Chicago right away. Linda didn't have a mom to help her so we tried to be the best substitutes we could. Before the baby was born, I bought an antique bassinet from the early 1900's. Vincent cleaned it up and painted it white. Then I decorated it with lace and beautiful fabric. After the baby was born and we knew it was a girl, I added pink ribbons.

After a while, Linda went back to work and hired someone to watch Michelle. Vincent and I visited them in Chicago often. When we were there, we took care of Michelle. I wanted her to be able to sign so she could communicate with us. I taught her how to sign "mommy" and "daddy" and "milk" and all kinds of things you teach little ones. She seemed to pick up signs quickly.

**Michelle, A Preschooler Interprets!**

One day when Michelle was in preschool, they had a special "Grandma and Grandpa Day." As we left, Linda told Michelle, "Don't forget. Take care of grandma." At school, I was watching the kids finger painting. The teacher asked me if I wanted "red" or "purple," but I didn't understand her. Michelle jumped in and began to interpret the teacher's question, using the signs I had taught her for the colors.

Later the children were sitting in a circle. Each grandparent had their grandchild on their lap. The teacher started counting and before I knew what was happening, Michelle began interpreting the numbers for me on her little fingers. She did it perfectly: 1, 2, 3 . . . 9, 10 in sign, just the way I had taught her to sign numbers. This little preschooler impressed me. I never told her to tell me what people were saying. She just did it automatically.

Then all the grandmas and the children got up and stood in a circle to do the "hokey pokey." Michelle was watching me. When they started singing "You put your right foot in, you put your right foot out," Michelle, picked up my right leg and put it in the circle. When it was time to put it back, she picked up my leg again, and put it back! When the music told us to turn around, she showed me exactly what to do. Amazing! This little four-year-old interpreting her preschool class for her grandma! Wow!

Later in the day the teacher was telling a story or playing a record. I'm not exactly sure since I couldn't hear it. It was too fast and Michelle couldn't interpret it. Michelle knew I couldn't understand anything. She climbed up onto my lap facing me and started mouthing all the words she was hearing, right in my face. I felt like I was back on Nana's porch with Paul. She was a special little preschooler. Believing she could do this was hard. When I got home, I told Linda and Paul what she had done and they were equally excited and impressed.

From the time Michelle was a baby, I always read stories to her. I never knew if she understood me, but she loved bedtime stories most of all. She always wanted me to go upstairs with her to read a story. Of course, I signed the stories while I was reading them.

### Michelle Wants to be Just Like Grandma

Michelle was so cute. In the morning she would ask me, "Grandma, what color dress are you wearing today?" I would answer, "Pink" and she would say, "Okay, I'm going to wear pink, too." If I told her "Brown," she would say, "I'm going to wear brown too." Michelle and I had a special bond. Sometimes Linda would ask Michelle, "What do you want for breakfast?" Before answering, Michelle would ask me what I wanted for breakfast. Then she would want whatever I wanted. If I wanted toast, she wanted toast too.

Once when Michelle was about five, I was sitting in the back with her while Linda was driving. Michelle said to me, "I wish I were Deaf." She signed that she wanted to be the same as me, Deaf. I told her, "You know, Michelle, you would miss music if you were Deaf." She didn't have an answer but I could see her little mind was thinking about it.

### Michelle—Proud to Know Sign Language

When I visit the children in Chicago, I walk them to the school bus stop. Once when we got there, I saw Michelle's friends asking her questions. I asked Michelle what her friends were saying. She told me her friends asked her if her grandma was Deaf. They asked if she knew how to sign and Michelle told me she said, "Yes, some." I could see Michelle was proud she knew some sign language. When I asked her to tell me what they were saying, of course, she answered me in sign. I could see she was showing off for her friends. She signed to me, "The kids asked me if you were Deaf and I said yes." I was so proud of her and it was clear she was very proud of herself too.

### Vinnie—the Next Grandchild

Vinnie was next. He's a nonstop talker. Sometimes Paul looks at him and says, "He looks so cute when he talks, especially with all his facial expressions." I said to Paul, "You know, that's exactly what you did while you were growing up. I feel like I have you back again, right in front of my eyes." Paul was shocked. He didn't have any idea his son was following in his footsteps.

Vinnie is an adorable, sweet, little boy. It's hard to explain his personality. He's always willing to share things. Ever since he was a tiny baby, Vinnie has had this stuffed animal, Eeyore. Once when the children were ready to go to bed, Vinnie lost Eeyore. He was hysterical. We looked inside and outside the house but couldn't find it. Eventually we found it in one of the small closets. I have a feeling he put it in there to protect it and then forgot he put it there.

When Vinnie was about three years old, his favorite animals were dinosaurs. He had pictures of dinosaurs on a wallpaper border in his room. Paul would ask him to tell me their names and he knew them all. Some of them were humongous long words. I could barely lipread them and I certainly couldn't spell them. Vinnie couldn't spell them either, of course, but he knew them all. I was quite impressed with a little three-year-old knowing so much. Vinnie used to call these dinosaurs "my guys." He thought of them as his friends.

He's seven now and he still loves to read books about dinosaurs. He's positive he wants to be an archeologist when he grows up. I believe him. His interest in dinosaurs has been consistent since he was three or four year's old. He can go into his room, all day, and play with his dinosaurs. He has so many books and pictures and toy dinosaurs in his room, I can't even count them.

### Lunch at School with Vinnie and Michelle

Recently, Vinnie and Michelle wanted me have lunch with them at school, on the same day. Michelle had lunch earlier so I joined her first. We went to the school cafeteria, got on line for lunch and sat and chatted, in sign.

Then I went to Vinnie's class. He introduced me to his teacher and carefully fingerspelled the teacher's name for me. Then, Vinnie and I went together to the cafeteria and got on line. The lady at the cafeteria recognized me and was a little surprised I was having a second lunch. During lunch Vinnie fingerspelled all his friends' names for me. I was very proud of him.

**Dominic, Our Third Grandchild**

Dominic, 3 months old, signing "I Love You"

Of course, when Dominic was born, we went out to Chicago, to help Linda, like we did when each child was born. We went directly to the hospital. We didn't even stop at Linda and Paul's house. He was the cutest looking baby. He looked quite different from Linda and Paul's other children. He had blond hair and blue eyes. Vincent asked, "Are you sure that baby is yours, the one with blond hair and blue eyes?" We kept thinking,

"It can't be ours." When the doctor came, we asked "Is that the Pizzo baby?" It was.

After a while his blue eyes turned hazel. When he was a week old, he started sucking his two middle fingers. You know, some babies suck their pinkies or their thumb. Dominic sucked the middle two fingers which makes the "I love you" in sign. He still does it. We took his picture doing the "I Love You" and sent it to the "Silent News" which is a nationwide Deaf newspaper. I have a Deaf friend from Pennsylvania who teaches ASL to hearing students. She saw his "I Love You" picture in the Silent News and made copies for her students!

Vinnie and Dominic used to depend on Michelle to interpret for them. Poor Michelle. She's always telling me what they're saying. Now that they're older, I can understand them better. Vinnie signs a little bit. To my surprise, he is starting to fingerspell.

**A Special Christmas at Home with Our Grandchildren**

One of the best Christmas' we ever had was a snowy night in New Jersey with the grandchildren. My brother and his family were also visiting. We were all sitting by the window watching the snow and waiting for Santa Claus. Santa Claus suddenly appeared standing near the railing of the roof of the garage. It looked like a scene from a movie. Wow! The children still talk about that. It could not have been more perfect. The grandchildren were enchanted. They ran outside and were enthralled to see Santa Claus standing on the roof.

We have a traditional Christmas food in our family, pignolatta. First, you saute sausage, spinach and onions in olive oil. Then you roll out dough into a huge rectangle. Roll the sausage mixture up in the dough, turn it into a huge spiral, and bake it. Paul makes it for his family in Chicago. Karen is also carrying on the tradition here in New Jersey.

Linda and Paul; grandchildren: l-r: Vinnie, Dominic, Michelle

# CHAPTER 9.

# I BECOME AWARE OF DEAF CULTURE

### The Opera

When I graduated from school, my aunt and my mom gave me what they thought was an exciting present, tickets to the opera. We wore our best clothes and went into Manhattan for the big event. I saw the cast making funny faces and gesturing with their arms. Maybe they thought I enjoyed seeing the costumes and staging but I couldn't help thinking, "I can't hear anything and I have no idea what's happening. " My aunt and mom turned and asked, "Are you enjoying yourself?" "Sure, thanks so much" I said. Of course, inside I was feeling disappointed. It was a weird experience. When I look back on it now, I think it's outrageously funny and sad, too.

My son, Paul, once dated a young woman who was an opera singer. Once, he invited us to see her in "The King and I." I have to be honest, I felt almost like time had stood still. It was like being at the opera again with mom and my aunt. I must admit, my husband, Vincent, and I did get some pleasure because we knew Paul's girlfriend was singing. Also since we knew something about the story, we could follow it a little. Just knowing somebody on the stage was kind of fun and we enjoyed the staging and the scenery.

It's amazing how times have changed. Back then I thought it

was okay. Today I would never put up with it. Nowadays, for example, if I turn on the TV and it's not closed captioned, I just turn it off. If I go to a movie and it's supposed to be open captioned and it's not, I'll just walk out. I can't bear to not understand. I can hardly believe I've lived long enough to experience open captioned movies, captioned television, and interpreted theater. It feels like a miracle happened in my lifetime. The young "me" willingly went to the opera and understood nothing. The older "me" goes to movies and theater and experiences the arts in a way I never dreamed possible.

### Working Again

While my children were in school, I was a full time mom and homemaker. After they were grown, I felt ready for full time work and interviewed for a job as a key punch operator. In those days, we never thought about having an interpreter for a job interview. The lady had a heavy German accent but moved her mouth carefully so I could lipread.

The interview seemed to go smoothly. She asked about my experience and the kind of key punch work I had done. When the interview was over, she asked, "Did someone bring you here?". I replied, "No, I drove here in my own car." She was stunned. Then she asked if I had children. I replied, "Oh yes, I have a Deaf husband but I have three hearing children." Again shock appeared on the lady's face. She had never met a Deaf person and didn't know anything about Deaf people. Then she asked me if I had a dog and I told her I did. I never figured out why she asked me about my dog.

She also wanted to know if people understood me when I went shopping. I told her, "Well, sometimes they don't understand me, so I write. Sometimes one of the children interprets for me." She seemed to accept that. No one had ever asked me questions about my being Deaf. I felt uncomfortable, but answered her questions and she hired me. I worked there eight years. My co-workers were kind and my boss was lovely. She was quite sensitive to my needs. Since there were no interpreters and no

TTY's, my co-workers were always willing to call the children for me or accept phone calls from them.

In 1996 when I chaired the Fashion show, I invited a few people from my job. I wanted them to know what Deaf people could do. A group of them came including my boss. Later, she sent me a card saying what a great job we had done and how impressed she was. I think, just from that experience, she learned that Deaf people can do many things.

**Caught Between Two Worlds . . . Hearing and Deaf**

Often the family comes over for special events, like birthdays or holiday celebrations. We always sit around the big table in the family room. If I have my Deaf friends at my home along with my hearing family, I'm just not comfortable. I don't know where to put myself. I don't know whether to be with Deaf people or with my hearing family.

I find myself constantly moving between my Deaf friends and my hearing family. Sometimes the Deaf people are talking and I have to explain what's happening to my hearing family. Then I'm with my hearing family and I have to explain what's going on to the Deaf people. One example that comes to mind was mom's funeral. The hearing relatives and friends sat in one room and the Deaf people sat in another. I didn't know where I belonged so I just rotated back and forth between them. I noticed that Judy Jonas, a hearing interpreter and friend, stayed with my Deaf friends. She knew my Deaf friends better than she knew my hearing relatives.

Other times when my hearing relatives and my Deaf friends are together at my house, I spend more time with my Deaf friends than with my hearing family. I have no idea how my family members feel about my doing that. It may depend on the number of people involved. For example, if I'm having a big party, a big Deaf crowd and a big hearing crowd, then everything is fine. But if it's a small group, here in the house, like Christmas or holidays, it's a little different. Sometimes I invite several Deaf couples, and the family. I always ask my hearing children or my brother (who lives in Long Island), "Do you mind if I invite some of my Deaf friends?" My children and brother always say, "Of course, sure, just go ahead." I don't think they mind if I join the Deaf group. The hearing relatives don't communicate with the Deaf people much at all. We just sit separately and do our own thing.

If it's just Vincent and me and my hearing relatives, this is what often happens. Vincent sits at one end of the table. I sit at the opposite end, facing him. Poor Vincent. He always looks bored. I can just see him, looking around. I try to catch, by lip-reading, what the various hearing relatives are saying and I'll ask them, "What's going on?" But Vincent just sits there quietly. When I catch his eye, he gently lets me know he's bored and he doesn't know what to do and sometimes I'm feeling the same way. Often we'll sign back and forth to each other from opposite ends of the table. We have a totally different and private conversation while all these hearing people around us are having their conversations. The hearing people don't know what we're saying and we don't know what they're saying. Amazing, isn't it?

## My Sister's Granddaughter, Nicole, A Natural Signer

Strange how things happen. None of my siblings or parents ever learned to sign, but my sister's granddaughter Nicole is a fluent ASL signer. I remember the first time she visited us from California. She was two years old. Something about her made me decide to teach her to sign. When she was five years old, she came again and I bought her the Linda Bove "Sesame Street" book. Almost from the moment she arrived, we sat together and went through every page. We started with the signs for animals and went through every sign. I thought she'd be bored by the second or third page, but she stayed interested, late at night. Imagine, she was only five years old and had intense interest and patience!

Many people stayed at our house because they had come for pop's 80th birthday. This little five-year-old was sleeping with my sister on the floor. Nicole couldn't stop signing. The house was dark, but Nicole just kept signing away! Everything I had taught her! My sister couldn't sleep because Nicole couldn't stop signing. When she was nine, she and my sister visited again. Again, we went shopping together and we kept practicing all the ASL colors: blue, pink, yellow, etc. I turned off my voice and showed her the sign for everything we saw. She soaked up the signs like a sponge.

She flew here another time, all by herself, when she was around eleven years old, and, again we stayed up way past midnight practicing signs together. After that she constantly begged her mom and dad to let her go visit her Aunt Rose in New Jersey. Finally they let her come when she was around fourteen or fifteen, and wow! When she first got here, she had forgotten much of what she had learned. Within a couple of hours, she was back to ASL. She could sign with me in the restaurant. She interpreted for me at the restaurant when the waitress took our order. I was so proud of her. She signed ASL so smoothly. My sister was thrilled too. My sister talks with her other grandchildren about me. They love to hear stories about my growing up Deaf.

Nicole is now seventeen. She's still in high school and works part time in an office, and I haven't seen her for a while. I miss her. I've encouraged her to be involved with Deaf people in the future. I hope she'll become an interpreter. But she has a boyfriend now and is busy with "boy things." She's not really keen on thinking about her future! I know if she visits again, we'll get back into ASL. Her skills might be rusty but I'm sure she'll remember when we start signing together. Her facial expressions while she signs are awesome. She's a natural signer.

### Getting Involved in the Deaf Club, North Jersey Community Center for the Deaf (NJCCD)

While we were living in Fair Lawn, I had heard about the Deaf club, NJCCD, but I was busy raising my children. I didn't know much about the club but occasionally Vincent would go to a meeting. I was not going to hire a baby sitter to take care of the kids so we could go together. The only baby sitter I ever used was my mother but we would use her to spend time with our friends.

Eventually the children were old enough to take care of themselves at home, so I started going to the Deaf club. I remember exactly what happened the first time I went. The meeting went right over my head. I understood nothing. This happened for quite a while. I couldn't figure out what was happening and asked a friend, "What are they were talking about?" My friend patiently explained the rules and policies. Eventually I started to get interested.

I think what helped me improve and understand what was going on, was the Adult Basic Education Program for the Deaf. It helped build my confidence. At the time, the NJCCD's Women's Auxiliary (WA) was already established, but I didn't want any part of it. At the meetings I kept hearing everyone talk about the WA and the women kept encouraging me to join. As my confidence increased, I started going to the WA meetings and I became more involved. Deaf role models brought me in, took me under their wings and helped me. It's hard to name them all: Lucy Foti, Sheila Lenner, Matilda O'Klock, Frances Hearne. They were way ahead of me but they led me into the WA and nurtured me. When I began to get involved, Fran was the President of the WA. When I started to attend meetings regularly, I just observed. I just couldn't seem to understand how they handled money or their finances. I was totally overwhelmed. I wondered how they knew so many things. It was just beyond me. After a while, I started to love the WA. Before I knew what was happening, they elected me secretary. Things just snowballed from there.

### Fair Lawn Adult Basic Education Program (ABE) Changes My Life

Raising my children here in Fair Lawn was quite an experience, but when the Fair Lawn Adult Basic Education (ABE) Program for the Deaf started in 1978, I was so excited! I was in the first group of students who registered when Janice Honig and Judy Jonas started the program at the Community School. During its first year, almost 100 Deaf adults enrolled. It was the first free literacy program for the Deaf in New Jersey. I had been out of school for many years, raising my family during the years without TTYs and without closed-captioned TV. I felt rusty and wanted to improve my reading and writing skills. I knew I needed it.

I had Deaf friends, but they were scattered all over the place and keeping in touch with each other was hard for us. We would visit back and forth but making arrangements was almost impossible. We had to drive back and forth to visit one another. Without a TTY and captioned TV, I was very isolated in Fair Lawn. When the ABE Program for the Deaf opened, I couldn't wait to get started. My friends were there. All of them. We enjoyed seeing each other and it was a place we could see each other every week and learn simultaneously.

I felt rusty when I first started. I felt ignorant about spelling and anything connected to English. I knew I was competent in my Deaf world, using ASL, but English was hard for me. But I stuck with it. While many of my Deaf friends dropped out, I just kept going. I was persistent. I remember I took some tests. I failed. I knew I failed and all of my friends passed. Their level was way above mine and I felt like I had gone back to kindergarten. Also, I was confused. I thought, "Me? I had always been a good student as a child. I had earned an Arista award. I still had my Arista pin. How could I fail the tests so badly?"

One day I approached Judy and Jan and said, "This can't possibly be me. I should be with the other group, with my friends. I feel like I should be up there with them." In fact, I was right. I did belong with my friends. I had not finished the test. I had worked very slowly because I was afraid that I would make a mistake. My score showed I finished only part of the test. Everything I had done was correct. Jan and Judy moved me into the other group with my friends. Everything was fine after that. I was just working slowly. I never missed a class. I kept going every week. Then, the class met two nights a week, not one night like now. I could go Wednesday and Thursday and I did; I felt myself improving every week.

Through the ABE Program I got involved in a special Adult High School where I could earn a high school equivalency diploma. For part of the requirements, I had to go to a mayor and council meeting at Borough Hall. Judy volunteered to interpret for me, because in those days no Americans with Disabilities Act (ADA) existed to require the town to provide an interpreter. Later, when I went to the Adult High School graduation ceremony, with several other Deaf classmates and an interpreter, I got a real Diploma! I was proud of myself and my Deaf classmates. My good friend Stanley Teger, who is now gone, was in my graduating group. Shortly after that, Jan and Judy hired me as a Teacher's Aide and I've been one for twenty years. It's been an incredible and challenging experience for me.

### From Student to Teacher

About ten years ago, the Fair Lawn Community School was looking for a replacement for their ASL teacher, and I got the job. I was frightened to teach hearing people, but I was willing to try. One day, a student asked me about my growing up in the hearing world. I was telling them my experience in the hearing school where I learned nothing for two years because I sat in the back. I was amazed when one of my students said, "Rose, you used to sit in the *back* of the class, but now you are standing in *front* of the class teaching hearing students!" Wow, how times have changed!

### Union County College (UCC)

When I was working at the Fair Lawn Deaf Program ABE Program, Union County College (UCC) interpreting students often came to observe. I was impressed with their interest in becoming interpreters. While I was growing up, I never had interpreters for many important events in my life, like my wedding, going to a doctor or my kid's school meetings. I never felt I could have a full conversation with hearing people. An interpreter would have made a big difference! These interpreting students were going to work in many different environments and allow Deaf people to communicate with the hearing world. Wow!

Lauren Kafka was a student taking sign language classes somewhere else and came to observe the Deaf students at the ABE Program. I could see her talking, not signing, with Phyllis Rosenberg, the hearing teacher. When she first started, she knew only a few signs. Poor thing, she was so awkward! Phyllis would explain a sign here and there to her, but Lauren was not involved in the class, she was just observing. I was busy teaching, but I could see Lauren was stiff as a board. She just didn't know how to communicate in sign. After a while, she started to sign a little bit to the students. If a student didn't understand her, I would help her out. She came every week and never missed a class. Gradually, her signs began to improve and I noticed she was beginning to warm up with the Deaf students.

I suggested she apply to UCC to learn more but I didn't push it. I could see she didn't feel ready. One night, she came to class and told me she had registered at UCC. I was thrilled for her. I felt sure she could do it and I told her. She found her first semester very difficult and asked if I would tutor her. I agreed she could come to my house to practice what she was learning in her classes. Together we would practice exactly how to make the word, the sign, the hand shape, the fingerspelling, everything. I would help her with the facial grammar and facial expressions required for ASL. She wanted to do it perfectly. Often I would sit behind her and, at night, we could watch our reflections in the window. Lauren was a very serious student but we had fun. She didn't miss a week of tutoring. We did it for quite a while and, through those sessions, we became friends. Unfortunately, Lauren never got to finish at UCC. Her husband's job transferred him to California. But she's still involved in the Deaf community and now she's going to an Interpreter Training Program at Pierce College in California. She told me recently she'll be interpreting Deaf Fest at Disney Land. I was so excited for her.

After my experience with Lauren, I became involved with

more UCC students and got involved in some UCC Deaf Culture events. I started going to the UCC ASL Festival every year. Now I wouldn't miss it. I've learned so much about Deaf history. I always thought, for example, ASL was broken English. Now I know ASL is our language and it's a real language. I loved socializing with the hearing UCC students who were learning ASL. I opened up the NJCCD meetings and events to UCC students. They knew if they came to an NJCCD event, they could find me. I would introduce them and make them feel comfortable and welcome in the Deaf community.

### I Win A UCC Award

One year I didn't go to the UCC ASL Festival, because I went to Italy to visit my family. One night, while I was at the hotel in Italy, Karen was talking to Nancy in New Jersey. My sister, my cousin and other relatives were in the hotel room. I was curious what they were talking about. Suddenly everyone in the family started laughing and I asked, "What's going on." The only answer I got was, "Wait a second." I said, "No, I want to know." I kept pestering them to tell me what was happening and they kept saying, "No, no, no, just wait, Karen will tell you." I was getting angry because everybody knew what was going on and I didn't. They couldn't stop laughing. Karen finally hung up. All the relatives were still laughing. I was furious.

After she hung up, Karen said, "Did you miss something on April 12?" I said, "Well, yes, there was an ASL Festival at UCC but I missed it." Karen said, "You missed something important, you know. You got an award, mom." I looked at her and I said, "What? What kind of award did I get? Are you crazy?" I said, "Say this again. Who got an award?" Karen repeated, "UCC gave you an award, ma." My brain froze. I had no idea what she was talking about. I'm thinking, "What? Me? An award? Impossible" I was numb. I didn't know what to do and I was confused. I couldn't imagine why they would give me an award. Later as we were riding on one of the buses, everyone on the bus started clapping. Karen must have told everybody about my award. But

I was still in a muddle. I couldn't figure out why UCC gave me an award.

After I got home, Lauren explained I won the Claudia Parson's Award. It is given to people who have been involved in the Deaf community and have encouraged UCC Interpreter Training Program and Deaf Studies students. I won the award because I made the UCC students feel comfortable at the Fair Lawn Deaf Program and at the NJCCD meetings. I had done a lot to help UCC students feel welcome in the Deaf world. I asked "How did the people at UCC know about me?" Her answer was, "Everybody knows you. They know you from the Fair Lawn Deaf Program and from NJCCD. Five hundred people knew you won the award although you weren't there to accept it." I wished mom and pop had been alive to see me get the UCC award. They would have been proud of me.

# CHAPTER 10.

## SYMBOLS OF DEAF CULTURE

**Doorbell Ringing Dog**

Once my Deaf friends and I were playing cards. It was cold that evening and Nellie had to go out. I opened the door and let the dog out and closed the door. We totally forgot Nellie. At around 11 or 11:30, we saw the lights flashing from the outside doorbell. We wondered, "Who the heck is ringing the doorbell at 11:30 at night?" It was Nellie! I opened the door and Nellie was jumping up and down, delighted to see me. Somehow, she figured it out. She jumped high enough to reach the bell and eventually rang it. It happened not once, but repeatedly. Nellie learned how to ring the doorbell! My friends were hysterical about that. They thought I should put her on TV.

**In the Hospital**

In the early '80's I needed to go to the hospital for minor surgery. I didn't have a hearing relative or anybody with me to interpret and didn't think about asking the doctor questions. I just accepted what the doctor said and scheduled the surgery.

When I got ready to go to the hospital, Judy Jonas lent me her portable TTY. Then, we only had a huge old model 15 TTY at home. Small portable TTY's were new and easy to use in the hospital. Vincent had to stay home and watch the children but with the portable TTY, I could call him from the phone near my bed. It was the first time in my whole life I had a conversation using the TTY with my husband and the children. When I used the TTY in the hospital, about fifteen nurses came into the room to watch. They couldn't believe their eyes and didn't understand how it worked. I explained to them how I could use the phone with the TTY to communicate with my children and husband. It was a fabulous experience.

With Judy's help I had a TTY in the hospital, but I felt the hospital should have their own. I wrote a letter to Senator Bill Bradley asking him to do something about requiring hospitals to make TTY's available for their Deaf patients. After all, hearing patients all have phones. Deaf patients can't use the phone without a TTY, so the hospital should provide equal access. He responded to me saying how he hoped in the future hospitals would have TTYs. Well, now it's the year two thousand. It took a long time for it to happen. They passed the ADA in 1990-91 and now they require hospitals to have TTYs for Deaf patients.

**Closed Captioning TV**

Sometime in the early 80's, captioned television began. Before that, there was nothing. If my family was watching television, I imagined what the actors were saying. I would imagine, for example, that a man or a woman were falling in love. It was the same as going to the movies when I was growing up. I didn't know any better and thought it was just fine. Later, when my children and I were watching TV, I would ask the kids "What are they crying about?" and they would tell me. Maybe they would tell me something briefly, like, "They're fighting" or "This one doesn't like that one. That's why they're crying."

When captioning started in the early 80's, we had to buy a special device called a decoder. It cost $250. It seems expensive but it was worth every penny. We didn't mind spending $250, because we could finally understand television. If the decoder broke, which often it did, we had to go buy another one for $250. Then, ten years later, in the early 90's when they passed the ADA, new TV's had to have the decoder chip built into it. That meant that any new television could show the captions and we didn't need to buy anything special.

When captioning first started, I remember, NBC was the only station with captioning. Then ABC started captioning some of their programs. We didn't care what was on. We would watch anything on NBC or ABC with captions. Vincent and I would channel surf to find a captioned show. We didn't care if it was good or bad. If they captioned it, we would watch it.

They now caption most shows, but not all. The laws are changing. Soon I'll be able to turn on any station and see the captions. What a difference from when I was growing up!

With captions, for the first time in my life, I could watch the news and know what was going on in the world. Hearing people got most of their news from television. Before captions, I could only get news from the newspapers or magazines. I would see people on the TV but I never understood the story. With captioning, I totally knew what was going on. Wow! I'm still waiting for captioned local news. I still have to read local news in the newspaper.

### Smoke Alarms

A long time ago we put smoke alarms in our house. But I would call them "hearing" smoke alarms because they were smoke alarms that made noise. I was told they sounded like a siren. If Vincent and I were sleeping, we wouldn't have heard them. But we had hearing children, and we knew if there was a fire in the house, in the middle of the night, the children would hear the alarm.

After the kids grew up and left home, we were aware that these smoke alarms were not very helpful. I heard there were strobe smoke alarms so that if there was a fire, a very bright light, a strobe, would flash and we would see it. They cost about $100 each. "Hearing" smoke alarms cost about five or ten dollars, but the strobe alarms were quite expensive. We put off buying them because they were so expensive. Our daughter, Karen, was concerned about us not having proper smoke alarms and bought two strobe alarms for us. We were thrilled to have them. We put one in our bedroom and the other in the basement because we were concerned about the furnace.

A Deaf women in town, Anne Roth, had a hearing daughter. The daughter was concerned about the Deaf families not having strobe alarms. She called the Fire Department and told them there were Deaf people living in town who didn't have strobe alarms because they were so expensive. The firemen chipped in and donated strobe alarms for two Deaf families. They asked me to help deliver the strobe alarms to them. When I went to their houses, the people were surprised and excited to learn they were free. Soon after, the Fire Department received an anonymous donation to buy ten more. In addition, the Knights of Pythias raised enough money to give away an additional eight. I've been involved in delivering all of the alarms to these Deaf families because, as a Deaf person, I can easily communicate with them.

One family here in town is a hearing family with a Deaf son. They wanted their Deaf son to have the strobe alarm in his room, so one of the donated alarms was put up in his room.

I'm thrilled the Fire Department got involved in helping the Deaf families here in Fair Lawn. It shows tremendous sensitivity. Things are getting better and better as we move into the twenty first century.

### Fair Lawn Police and TTY's

I've been living in the same house in Fair Lawn for close to forty years. Over these years, there were about ten Deaf families living in town. One of these men was Lee Brody. Lee was a genius and was responsible for making TTY's available for Deaf people. He gave each family a free TTY. Back then, about thirty years ago, TTY's were huge big, ugly things. They also made a lot of noise. We didn't care because with these TTY's, we could finally communicate with each other smoothly and easily. We didn't have to go driving back and forth to each other's house.

As the years passed, TTY's became smaller and eventually portable. Lee told the Fair Lawn Police Department they should have TTY's because it was the only way Deaf people could contact them. The police were not the slightest bit interested. They turned him down every time. I remember thinking, "I have a TTY. Why doesn't the police station have one?" So I went over to the police station and tried to convince them but I couldn't communicate with them effectively and I just dropped it.

My close friend Phyllis had a daughter, Tracey, who worked for the phone company. I told Tracy how I felt the Fair Lawn Police should have a TTY for the Deaf people that lived in town and she offered to help me. She told them ATT was willing to donate a TTY to the Police Department. They accepted it right away. Then we went over, with the TTY, and taught them how to use it.

I have wondered why Tracey could convince the Police Department to have a TTY but Lee and I couldn't. Maybe because she gave them a free TTY. I think when Lee and I tried to convince them, the police didn't understand how important it was for Deaf people to have contact with the Police Department. Now they are a bit more aware. Occasionally the Police Department contacts me, through the TTY, to make sure that they still knew how to use it. They also want me to contact them, occasionally, to make sure they know what to do when they get a call.

The last time the police called me, on the TTY, they were very concerned. I was really quite impressed because it seemed like, in the past, they really didn't care. I'm happy they call to check that everything is working properly, that I can read them and they can read me. They also called to check that 911 was working and, of course, I was willing. They asked me to call 911. Wow! Everything went through the computer. They knew my address right away. I was tremendously relieved and thanked them for taking the trouble to make sure the system was working. There are more Deaf families living in Fair Lawn now. There are some young Deaf families that have recently moved here. I feel good the police are concerned about everybody's safety and they take the trouble to check that the system is working.

### Interpreted Theater

I go to many interpreted shows now and enjoy them enormously. I can follow the story, see the staging and everything is perfect. Recently, I went to an interpreted show, a Passion Play of "The Jesus Story." For the first time, watching the story through the interpreter, I had an understanding about how Christ and Easter are connected. The information was clear, through the interpreter, and exciting. I went back, to see it again, the following night.

The same weekend as the Passion Play, I went to an interpreted performance of "Joseph and His Technicolor Dream Coat." Again, because of the interpreters, I could understand the bible story. I realized how much I had missed as a child. Although I was raised in a Catholic family and attended church, I never understood much about my religion. We never had interpreted church services or shows. Unfortunately, my religious knowledge was superficial based on the actions, never the words.

Here I am, in my mid 60's, finally beginning to understand religion because of these interpreted performances. I guess hearing children go to shows all the time and learn from them. My time has finally come! I can't believe I've lived long enough to enjoy and understand religion through the theater. Now I know why people like the theater so much. Now that I can understand it, so do I. Wow!

### Staying Connected by Phone

My sister Frances and I were quite close growing up. She took care of me a lot. After she got married, she lived in Queens for a while, but because of her husband's job, she had to move to California. Mom worried about how Frances and I would stay in touch so mom bought Frances a TTY for Christmas. Frances used to say to me, "The TTY is God's gift to us. It gives us a way to communicate. The miles aren't important. The TTY connects us."

When my brother bought his house in Huntington, Long Island, mom also bought him a TTY for Christmas, so he could call me. Mom never had a TTY of her own! If mom needed to tell me something, she would do it through my children. They would interpret. I was never sure if the kids told me the whole story. Maybe they only told me what was important. First they would have a long private conversation with grandma, and if there was something mom needed to tell me, she would do it through the kids.

Perhaps mom didn't get her own TTY because English was not her first language. Even writing English was hard for her. She didn't know how to type. So typing in English on the TTY was a double problem. It was easier to ask my children to interpret for her.

When the kids were too young to use the phone, she couldn't use them as interpreters. So, instead, she would call a neighbor to tell me things. We actually had a system. She would call a neighbor once a week just to make sure everything was ok and the neighbor would tell her. Can you imagine that? This was before TTY's were invented.

When mom moved to Fair Lawn, I saw her constantly. If she needed to reach me, she would call my neighbor, and I would go over to mom's house. The telephone relay service, started in the early 90's, made a big difference. I taught mom how to use the relay service. She was nervous, in the beginning but after she learned how, she was comfortable using it. She would use it frequently if she needed something at the store or wanted me to come over because she wasn't feeling well, or she needed to arrange a doctor appointment. The relay really made things a lot easier for us. We finally had phone communication that worked. Mom didn't use relay just to call and chat with me. She called me if she needed something and I could help her.

Relay has made a tremendous difference in my life. I can call a doctor. I can order pizza. I can order from catalogues. It has made life so much better for Deaf people and for me especially. So many of my friends tell me that they are so appreciative and grateful for the relay service. We don't have to depend on our children or neighbors to make calls for us. What a difference! We can do things on our own now and not have to impose on others.

Nurses call me to remind me of my doctor's appointment. They seem very comfortable using the relay service. Ten years have gone by now and people are getting used to it. There are still those who don't know about the relay but most people seem able to use it.

### Hiring an Interpreter at Family Events

Recently I talked to my sister, on the TTY, about the family reunion coming up this summer. I said, "You know, I was thinking, times have changed. Deaf culture involves a lot of things nowadays. I'm thinking maybe we should have an interpreter for a few hours at the family reunion this summer."

She answered quickly, "Absolutely, for sure. That's a great idea. I'd be willing to chip in and maybe our brother, Vinny, would too. I'll call him and talk about it. We should do that." I questioned her further to make sure she knew it would cost money. "Are you willing to pay?" She said, "Sure and I bet Vinny will too."

If that happens, it would be the first time the family will pay to have an interpreter at a family event. Wow!

# CHAPTER 11.

## AN ENDING AND A NEW
## BEGINNING

**NJCCD Fashion Show 1996**

NJCCD's Fashion Show of 1996, sponsored by the Women's Auxiliary was the experience of a lifetime! People still talk to me about it. Of course, NJCCD had sponsored Fashion Shows before, but '96 was the Fashion Show I chaired. What a fantastic experience!

The Fashion Show was a fund raiser for our Deaf Senior Citizens. Three hundred fifty-two hearing and Deaf people came to the Fashion Show, many of them from out of town: Connecticut, New York and Pennsylvania. We raised $9,400 for the Senior Citizens. As of today we have about $13,000 sitting in the bank from the several Fashion Shows, most of it raised in 1996! People still ask me when we're going to have another.

The committee was the best! Each meeting would include a pot luck meal where we just had fun. We worked hard but the relationships that grew among us were special. Friendships developed and flourished at our committee meetings. Each of us had a specific job to do. One was in charge of the money. Someone else was responsible for the tickets. Another took care of the prizes. There were so many things to do! I tried to be creative and use the special talents of each committee member. The team worked hard and everybody had fun.

NJCCD's first Fashion Show was by Saks Fifth Avenue. Our second, the one I chaired, was from a group in Philadelphia called, "Journey Productions, The Musical Fashion Show." The event was outstanding for many reasons. Music was one of them. The store hired "Journey Productions" to provide the music and play constantly while the models were walking down the runway. Many hearing people told me the music was fabulous and added to the fun. Simultaneously, the interpreters interpreted the songs. Karen Kearns was in charge of the interpreting along with some Union County College intern interpreters, who did a little interpreting, for the experience. It was so neat.

The store brought their own gorgeous models, ages eighteen to senior citizens. They were all professionals wearing the latest fashions. At the end of the Fashion Show a singer invited us all to join her in the Macarena and the whole place went crazy. Everybody jumped onto the runway and danced the Macarena, hand motions and all! The place went wild. Imagine more than three hundred Deaf and hearing people doing the Macarena together. What an ending to an unforgettable event!

The prizes were incredible! Sheila Favara was the chairperson of the prize committee. They were incredibly creative and clever! They made ninety huge baskets filled with donations of brand-new prizes. Every basket had its own theme. For example, we had a whole basket filled with kitchen tools like a peeler, can opener and sponges. There was another basket of Italian foods such as canned tomatoes, pasta and Italian spices. One had bedroom items, like a clock or picture frame. Yet another was filled with cook books WA members had made especially for the Fashion Show. There was one huge basket filled with bathroom items: towels, powders, scented soaps and bath oils. The room was filled with these gorgeous baskets of fun.

Before the party we laid out all the donated prizes in my house. We then tried to figure out where each item would fit. It was so much fun. Just picture us saying, "OK. Let's see where this goes. This belongs in a bathroom." Then we'd hunt for all the donations that could go in a bathroom. Quickly, a whole basket was full to the brim with bathroom things. Or we'd have a bunch of pens, pencils, and fancy writing paper, so we'd fill another basket with stationery items. Every basket was decorated and colorful. Each was a treat. Everyone was impressed. They'd never seen such clever prizes.

People won prizes by bidding, Chinese auction style. I wanted everyone to be able to pick the prizes they wanted and not force people to take a prize they didn't want. At the beginning of the show, there were cups in front of each basket. People bought tickets to put in the cups near baskets containing things they wanted. If you liked things related to Italian food and pasta, you could put your name on your tickets in front of that basket. The person picking the prizes would be picking your name for prizes you wanted.

Grace's Werra's committee assignment for the Fashion Show was to sell candy. We wanted to use the money raised from candy sales to give away a fax machine as a door prize. Grace decided she wanted to give away three fax machines! The committee was hesitant about her selling enough candy, but Grace was confident she could do it. We gave her the go ahead. Wow! She did it. She sold the candy everywhere! She made enough money to pay for the candy, buy three fax machines, and still have two thousand dollars profit. We were so impressed!

When the modeling part of the show was over and it was time to start picking the prize winners, you could feel the excitement in the room. Picture ninety of these baskets, not on the edge of the room but on the edge of the runway. They filled the entire length of the runway. Everyone had been dying to get their hands on them all afternoon, while the models were showing the clothing. It was fabulous. It was such an clever idea. It wasn't on a table where you had to go in a big crowd to look. You could just go right up to the runway, at eye level, and look closely at these baskets, ninety baskets of gorgeousness. The hearing people were shocked that Deaf people could do such a creative job. I have to admit, I was also impressed with our committee. I was proud of us, as Deaf people, that we could do such awesome work.

Besides the magnificent prizes, we also had two unusual straw hats that were part of a fifty-fifty raffle. The committee was brilliant to have thought of this. I don't know what I would have done without them! Eileen Vandenburg made one of these incredible hats and Florence Sabo made the other. The straw hats were decorated with fifty single dollar bills in the shape of a fan. The dollar bills went around the edge of one hat. It looked like a pony tail of money. The other one was slightly different but had another set of fifty singles. People couldn't stop buying raffle tickets to win these exquisite hats. Each side of the room, around the runway, had their own raffle to win one of the hats. People wanted these hats so badly, we raised a fortune just on their raffle tickets. At one point, the raffle tickets were totally sold out and Lucy came up to me and said, "I need more tickets. Everyone wants to win my hat." Unfortunately, my responsibility was to keep the event moving but Lucy wanted me to make more tickets and I said, "No, we can't. We don't have the time. That's it. We have to stop." She pleaded with me and said people were desperate to buy more tickets. But I was in charge of the schedule and I knew we were never going to make it if we were selling more raffle tickets for the hats. I had to keep everything in order and keep the event moving according to plans. Otherwise, we would still be there!

In addition to all the prizes, everyone went home with a beautifully wrapped souvenir calculator. Charlotte Cole was able to get 350 of them through her daughter-in-law. The committee spent all day wrapping them for the guests, but it was worth the effort.

Another part of the Fashion Show fund raising was our WA cookbook. Nancy La Forte agreed to be chairperson of the Cookbook Committee. It was a humongous amount of work but she really jumped into it. We sent letters out to all the members asking them to send us recipes. Then we asked Lenny Amato to help us because he was an expert in layout and design. Louise Sahajian and Barbara Harucki proofread. It was a huge job editing the recipes.

Lenny Amato typed all the recipes, did the layout and turned it into a beautiful WA cookbook. What a challenge! We never thought the cookbook would be ready by the Fashion Show but we struggled along and it got done. We sold 225 of them for $5 each at the Fashion Show.

When people ask me if we have plans for another Fashion Show, I say, "Well, I just don't know." A woman called me two or three times because she wants us to have another. Someone from Brooklyn heard about it and called me to find out the date for the next one! Even the Deaf community in Florida heard about our Fashion Show. They said if we had another they were willing to fly up from Florida! Deaf people from Long Island told me they'd charter a bus. I know I can't do it again. I did it twice and I just I can't do it again. I'm sort of heartbroken about it. Unfortunately, the young members are not interested in doing it. We are still trying to encourage them to have another, but so far, we have not been successful.

It was such an amazing event. Even the hearing neighbors said it was the best fund raiser they'd ever attended. They couldn't stop talking about it because it was sensational. They told me they had been to many Fashion Shows, but they'd never been to anything like the one our WA put on. One person told me it was the best Fashion Show in the whole United States but, you know, that's an exaggeration, but it was a lovely event.

**Deaf Problem Solving**

In 1996 the Fashion Show Committee often held planning meetings at my house. One night, I noticed the basement door was open, so I locked it. I have a habit of locking it because I feel safer when it's locked.

Suddenly, in the middle of the meeting, the lights went out. The whole house got dark and I became frightened. I started looking for Vincent to help us. I walked past the basement door and then I said to myself, "Oh my God. I locked Vincent in the basement!" During our committee meetings, Vincent usually went down to his basement workshop to work on various projects. My poor husband was banging on the basement door for a long time but, of course, we didn't hear him. But he's clever. He knew how to get the attention of a group of Deaf people—visually. He simply turned off the circuit breakers and all the lights went out. That did it! I found him!

On a related topic, sometimes when my kids were fighting upstairs, and hollering and screaming, the dog would bark. Every dog we ever had would bark like crazy if the children were fighting. It seems Deaf people always find a way. Like Vincent throwing the circuit breakers to get our attention. Or the dog barking to let us know the kids were carrying on. There's always a way.

### The End of the NJCCD Women's Auxiliary (WA)

The Women's Auxiliary of NJCCD just celebrated their fifteenth anniversary. To celebrate, we threw ourselves a party. Louise Sahatjian was the chairperson and about ninety people came. As part of the entertainment, we talked about the history of WA and gave out prizes recognizing members for their hard work over the years. Unfortunately the fifteenth anniversary party was WA's final event. Sadly, we cannot find younger members to continue WA's work.

Nevertheless, we are proud of all the events we sponsored and the donations WA made to charities. We gave money to many parts of the Deaf community: the Midland Park High School Program for the Deaf; Access, the Barnert Hospital Mental Health Program for the Deaf and to a young woman from New Jersey who was competing in the Deaf Olympics. We often donated money to a family's favorite charity in memory of a loved one. WA sent money to help rebuild a Deaf school in South Carolina, after Hurricane Hugo and helped sponsor a trip to Poland so Deaf high school students could learn about the Holocaust. Every year, WA's money paid for the toys for the children at NJCCD's annual holiday party and paid for the magician who entertained them.

Unfortunately the WA is now gone. These special and timely donations will not happen anymore. We all felt so sad. At the end of the party, we sat around crying. It was a big part of our lives and we will miss the fun we had together planning and putting together fund raising events. Now we only have our memories and our pictures.

**The Division of the Deaf and Hard of Hearing (DDHH)**

The Division of the Deaf and Hard of Hearing (DDHH) is the state organization that helps Deaf and Hard of Hearing people in New Jersey. They have an Advisory Council of late deafened, Deaf, hard of hearing and hearing people to make recommendations to the Director. Soon after I went to the DDHH twentieth anniversary party, I started to become interested in attending the meetings of the Advisory Council. I was fascinated and saw many interesting discussions at the meetings. The first time I went to one of the Advisory Council meetings, one of the members, suggested that I put my name in to become a member. He said they need people "like me." I was just a guest and felt I didn't understood enough to be on the Council. I was definitely not ready but told him I would think about it although I was fascinated and inspired by the discussions I saw.

The experience reminded me of NJCCD and the Women's Auxiliary where I felt overwhelmed at first, but after a while I began to understand what was going on. Finally I agreed to let them put my name in to become a member and I was recently appointed, by the Governor, to be a member of the DDHH Advisory Council. The purpose of the Advisory Council of the DDHH is to improve the conditions of deaf and hard of hearing people in New Jersey and to give advice from a Deaf perspective. I know I can do that.

# CHAPTER 12.

## Comparisons . . . Then and Now

### Mom Goes to Italy. Pop Stays Home

A year after Vincent and I were married, mom went to Italy to visit her father. It was the first time in twenty-five years she had seen him. I'm not sure why, but Pop didn't go with her, possibly because of "family problems." He was an old-fashioned man and just didn't see any reason to go to Italy. But I think it was a shame he didn't go. His brothers came from Italy to visit and I guess that was good enough for pop. Maybe he didn't have the money to go or maybe he didn't want to spend the money. I don't know which but I do know, he never went.

Pop's idea of a "trip" was to travel with the senior citizens from his church, Saint Anne's. When he was in his 70's, he would go on day trips to Pennsylvania or New York. He didn't go anywhere far but to him it was a "big trip."

### My Trip to Italy

I never met any of my grandparents because they never came to America. They stayed in Italy. Shortly after mom died, in 1996, my sister Frances and I started talking about the possibility of going to Italy. A group of us decided to go together: me, my sister Frances, my cousin Frances, her daughter Lisa, and my daughter, Karen. We found Italy breathtaking and beautiful. We couldn't imagine why mom and pop ever left Italy to come to America! Of course, we realized they came to America for a better life.

When we arrived in Italy, all the first cousins from my mom's two sisters, were waiting at my aunt's house to greet us. I have twenty-nine first cousins in Italy. Here I have two: cousin Frances and cousin Rose, who lives in Detroit. It was exciting just seeing them all. When we got to the house, the first thing we saw was an enormous double door. Just inside the door was the tiniest narrow elevator I ever saw. Strange contrast, a huge door and a tiny elevator! All the cousins and mom's sisters were waiting outside the elevator for us. As the elevator door opened, they grabbed us, hugged us, kissed us and cried. I couldn't take eyes off my mom's sisters. I just couldn't believe it. These were my mom's sisters and I had never met them in my whole life. One of my aunt's name is Rose, named after my mother's mother. My family has seven Roses, all named after my grandmother.

Before we even sat, Aunt Rose said we must see Uncle Dante. We went into his bedroom, and saw Uncle Dante lying in his bed. He looked like he had stepped right out of "The Godfather." The sheets were up at his neck and his hands were folded at his chest. All five of us were there: cousin Frances, her daughter Lisa, my daughter Karen, my sister Frances, and me. One by one, we came forward and gave Uncle Dante a kiss. All he could do was stare at the five of us. He did not say a word. I felt like he was staring at me the most. He had his eyes fixed on me and I couldn't figure out why. I saw a picture on the dresser of my mom and Titsi. Poor Karen, when she saw the picture she started to sob because she loved her grandma so much. Uncle Dante didn't say a word. We tried to make small talk and said little things like, "Nice to see you. Are you okay?" Finally Aunt Rose came in and suggested we go back to the living room.

A little while later Uncle Dante asked his niece to get me. When my niece came out and said, "Uncle Dante wants to see you," I said, "Who me?" A little frightened, I went in and I looked at Uncle Dante and said, "Uncle Dante, are you okay?" I didn't quite know what to do so I began to rub his hands, but he still didn't say anything. He stroked my hand and continued staring at me. Eventually I left the room, saying, "I'll see you later." He never said a word to me. When I returned to the living room, everybody asked, "What did Uncle Dante say to you?" I said, "Nothing," and they all laughed. It seemed ridiculous to me. For the three days we were there, Uncle Dante sat in the wheelchair glaring at me. I never did figure out why.

### Communication at Home with My Family

All my life, communication kind of broke down. Frequently, the family would forget to tell me something. I would always have to ask somebody what was going on. Suppose I saw somebody crying or suppose I saw somebody laughing hysterically, I would have to ask, "What's going on? What are they laughing about?" Then somebody would tell me but I'd only get the short version.

While I was growing up, it happened often. Now, things have improved. For example, when the family has dinner together for the holidays, they realize I don't know what's going on. They're much more aware. They're aware of Deaf culture and they're aware of my needs as a Deaf person. Like, for example, recently we got together and communication was pretty good. Of course, it's not perfect and I still miss lots of things, but it's a big improvement over my childhood. My brother was sitting and talking. Suddenly I saw him realize I couldn't follow him, and he turned to me and he said, "I'm sorry." He then began to speak differently. He used facial expression and lip movements so I could understand him. I notice the difference now. Communication between us is much better. My siblings and family members see Deaf people on TV. They're aware of the Americans with Disabilities Act (ADA). I, too, have changed. I'm more assertive and I've made them aware of what I need. I've talked with them about Deaf culture, the ADA, and interpreters. I support Deaf culture and they hear me talking about it. They hear me talking about the Deaf World today and I'm not quiet anymore. The family has become more sensitive because of my assertiveness, especially my sister and brother.

### Communication . . .  Different Homes, Different Styles

I know as a child, I was generally a happy person. It's kind of strange. I remember feeling I didn't know what was going on but I didn't think anything was wrong. I thought it was normal not to understand. That was just part of my life. I just didn't understand and I thought it was O.K. I didn't realize it was not O.K. until I married Vincent. I was so excited. Vincent and I could sign with each other, in our own home. My whole life, while I was growing up, I had to be with hearing people. Finally, in my house, my home, I could communicate easily with my husband, morning, noon and night, twenty four hours a day. Wow!

Our Deaf friends and their children came to visit. We could communicate smoothly, day or night. It felt like we had almost entered a different universe. My hearing family was a very supportive family, but in our newly married life, communication was simple. Our Deaf friends could come over for dinner and we could just stay up talking all night. Of course, when I say "talking," I mean communicating in ASL. It was a very different experience from my growing up years in a hearing family. My husband and all of my Deaf friends became like family. I came from a loving hearing family but getting married to Vincent and having our Deaf friends over was the first time I had totally accessible communication, any time I wanted, in my own home.

About three or four years ago, I was invited to be a panel member at Mountain Lakes High School, as part of their Deaf Awareness Week celebration. Greg Hlibok, a Deaf young man from a Deaf family, and I were asked to describe our childhood experiences. A large audience of parents, teachers, students and other school professionals came to the presentation. Greg and I took turns describing our experiences. I explained what it was like growing up Deaf in a hearing family and he described his experiences growing up Deaf in a Deaf family. I explained, for example, that when I was a kid, I didn't understand much of what went on at home. He described how he had learned to sign as a baby and could communicate with his family and his Deaf relatives.

Greg and I had totally different childhoods. Not only was it an eye opener to the audience but even I was amazed at the differences in our stories. Many came up to us after our presentation and told us how impressed they were by our different lives, stories and experiences. Although I knew Greg slightly before we were invited to the presentation, we didn't plan what we were going to do. I think we were a perfect pair because our family lives were so different. Our school lives were also interesting and opposite from one another. In my classes, I spent a lot of time trying to learn how to talk. He was allowed to sign in school and concentrate on learning the subjects. It was an amazing experience both for us. The audience got a chance to see how different lives can be for a Deaf person growing up in a hearing family compared to a Deaf family. They also saw the differences in Deaf education in my generation compared with Greg's more recent experience.

**Hearing School Attitudes**

When my kids were growing up, they were not aware I was Deaf. I mean, they knew I was Deaf but we never talked about it. Our Deafness was just there. Times are different today. Back then, I would go to a school meeting and have a brief conversation with my children's teachers. It would be the most superficial, "Karen's doing fine." "Everything is great." "Nice to meet you." Compare that with my recent visit to my granddaughter, Michelle's pre school class, where the teacher was teaching the children how to sign songs.

Children see interpreters in their schools where Deaf students are mainstreamed. There is much more awareness about Deaf people today. When my children were growing up, we were there, but nobody tried to include us. For example, I volunteered in the cafeteria at Saint Anne's, but nobody ever talked to me. Nobody attempted to make sure I was involved with the other volunteer moms. I would clean up the tables, make sure the children were eating, but no other mom even tried to communicate with me. I would see all the other parents chatting but I was left out. I was by myself. When school was over, I went home. I always felt disappointed. I never felt involved or included.

I had just the opposite experience, in the 90's, at Michelle's pre school, We all went to the cafeteria for lunch together. Michelle was excited because I was there. Little Michelle interpreted to make sure I could participate. The children wanted to learn sign language from me. I showed them some signs, right there in the lunchroom. They quickly learned "boy" and "girl" and "mom" and "dad." Every kid in the class had their eyes on me. They were excited to learn from me and worked hard to copy my signs. I could tell they respected me as an expert on signs. Compared to my experiences at St. Anne's, where I came home disappointed, it was like being on another planet.

When my kids were growing up, there just wasn't anything special for Deaf people. Nobody paid much attention to or tried to involve us. Today I feel like I can participate in the hearing world. There are many things available to improve the lives of Deaf people. We have portable TTY's and relay services to easily call anyone any where every day of the year. Television programs are closed captioned. Deaf kids are mainstreamed in schools with hearing children, and many Deaf kids are going to mainstream programs near home.

I've been invited to speak about my life at these mainstream schools. Finally, I feel included! It's quite interesting and a whole different experience. Recently I was one of four Deaf people on a panel at Passaic County Vocational and Technical High School. The meeting was broadcast through satellites to students at three other schools in New Jersey. We told our stories. During the question and answer part, the kids asked us a lot of questions. Years ago, if I went to my kid's school, nothing happened. Nobody thought to ask me about my life. I was totally ignored. The world has definitely changed!

## Hearing People Mock Deaf People

While I was growing up, many people made fun of us because we were Deaf. They made fun of the noises we made. They made fun of us signing. But today things are different. There are laws like the ADA. There are Deaf people signing in television commercials. There are interpreters in theaters and in movies. Maybe all this exposure helps hearing people understand Deaf people better. Maybe they don't make as much fun as they used to.

I know I feel more comfortable in the hearing world than I did as a child. I always felt I had to watch myself when I was out in the hearing world. But now I feel things have changed so much. I feel more comfortable. If people look at me because they hear me talking or see me signing, I always smile at them. I feel very confident. In the past, I would never make eye contact with someone who was looking at me. I would keep my distance totally. But today I just feel relaxed about people catching my eye and watching me.

Life is very different today than it was when I was growing up. In general, things are better for Deaf people. We have closed captioned television. We have relay services for the telephone. I think those were hard and sometimes painful times. I remember feeling very sad and I remember crying a lot because people made fun of me.

Not too long ago, a UCC student interviewed me about Deaf culture and about being a Deaf person. She had a whole list of questions. One question asked, "If there was a magic pill that would make you hear tomorrow, would you take it?" I said, "No. I'm just fine the way I am. Life's much better than it was when I was growing up. I'm waiting for some other improvements to happen, but I'm comfortable being Deaf. I'm very happy with my identity as a Deaf person."

Today some Deaf people are getting cochlear implants. The same student asked me if I wanted to have a cochlear implant and I said, "No I'm just very happy the way I am. I don't need it. I accept myself as a Deaf person."

**Baby Talk**

When my kids were very little and learning to talk I never could understand their "baby talk." I accepted that. No hearing person was around to interpret what the children were saying. I never even thought about it.

However, with my grandchildren, I want to know what they're saying and I'm aggressive about it. Sometimes when I see them talking, I'll ask, "What are they saying?" Linda interprets for me and it's fascinating. Now I realize how much I missed of my own children's cute "baby talk" or adorable sayings. I had no idea how wonderful it was to "listen in on" children learning to talk. I love knowing how they put words and sentences together.

Times were different then. Today I make it my business to find out what the children are saying by asking Linda or Paul to interpret for me. Because I "hear" the adorable things they're saying, I feel like I'm much more involved in their lives.

I read many stories to my three grandchildren. Linda and Paul read to their kids and I know it's important. I didn't read many stories to my children when they were young. Back then, I didn't realize how important reading was and I didn't know how. I think I have read more stories with my grandchildren than I ever read to my own three kids!

Today, I'm older and wiser and I love reading to the grandchildren. My parents never read to me. Remember, my parents were Italian immigrants. They didn't read stories with me or my brother or sister. So I didn't grow up with the role model of parents reading to me.

**Sign Language With the Children . . . Then and Now**

It's interesting to compare what happened at my daughter Karen's cheerleading tournament long ago with what happens now. I think about my grandchild, Michelle, who interpreted for me in her preschool when she was only four. She made sure I knew what the teacher said and what the other grandmas were saying. The difference is amazing! Times were different when Paul was growing up compared to the world Michelle lives in. Linda, Michelle's mother, signed to Michelle from the time she was born. Linda felt that signing was important for Michelle. Michelle also saw Linda interpreting for me and Vincent since she was little.

When our children were young, it was quite different. Vincent and I did not try to teach the children to sign. We spoke to them. Most of my friends did the same and didn't sign with their kids. They talked to them. Everything was oral back then and we didn't think about teaching our kids to sign. Today, Deaf parents use signs with their hearing children from birth and expect their kids to sign to them. It's also easier to see signing out in the world today. Interpreters are in so many places—churches, hospitals, schools and on TV. Kids see that and are comfortable around people using sign language.

**Restaurants**

When Deaf people go to restaurants, communication with the waiters can be a little difficult. Often, because they do not understand our speech, we need to point to the menu. One restaurant experience I will never forget was in Baltimore. It was back in the early 1980's and we waited a while for the host to seat us. Eventually he got our attention to tell us our table was ready. He put us in the darkest corner of the restaurant. We felt like he was hiding us so nobody would see Deaf people in the restaurant. This wasn't the first time that happened.

Shortly after we were married, Vincent and I and some friends went away for the weekend to a country resort. The resort had lots of activities we could participate in: tennis, swimming, biking and things of that sort. When we went to breakfast, they stuck us in a totally separate house with no other people. We didn't complain. I guess we thought that being separated was okay. Now, I think it's disgusting but, at the time, I didn't know any better and I just accepted it.

After the incident happened in Baltimore, I did something

about it. Here's what happened. At the time, I was a student at the Adult Basic Education Program in Fair Lawn. I told my teachers, Jan and Judy, what happened in the restaurant. Both said, "If you didn't like that, you should complain." So I wrote the manager a letter complaining how they stuck us in a dark corner and saying how unhappy we were. I got an answer with a big apology. He promised he would never do that again. That's when I started learning about my rights as a Deaf person and started getting an education about Deaf culture. I began to stand up for myself as a Deaf person.

A few weeks ago, I went to a Deaf Expo on Long Island. Afterwards, a whole group of Deaf people went to a restaurant, The Schooner, near the bay. We asked the hostess for a table for seven. She was really hard to lipread. We had to repeat ourselves several times until she understood us. Often we ask for a round table so we can communicate more easily, but we forgot. When she called us, we saw she had given us a round table, right near the window and near the water where we could enjoy the view of the bay and the boats. The waitress was fabulous. She didn't sign but for some reason we could lipread her. Also, she used lots of gestures. We felt like the restaurant went out of its way to give us a round table near the window so we could enjoy the scenery and gave us a waitress that we could understand. After struggling with the hostess, communication was very smooth.

What a difference from the restaurant in Baltimore or the country resort. In the past, putting Deaf people in the back where they could hide them, was common for a restaurant. Over the years, Deaf people complained. Maybe the restaurants have learned. Also maybe the world is just more sensitive to Deaf culture so they put us where we can see. Maybe they're not embarrassed that we are in their restaurant. Times have definitely changed. The restaurant stories are a good everyday example.

I still hear some complaints, even today, about Deaf people in restaurants. We run into some problems that Vincent and I ran into years ago, with getting seated in dark corners, but definitely things are improving.

### Telling My Story

I told my brother Vinny and my sister-in-law Nancy what we're doing, how I'm signing my life story and Judy is interpreting it into a tape recorder. Nancy just could not believe how long we're taking. We've been getting together every week since January, soon after Judy's retirement. She asked me, "What are you guys talking about?" I answered, "Well I'm explaining about my life, about my being Deaf, about communication, about our bad times and our good times." She was fascinated and told me she can't wait to read it. She showed me a book she had started writing for her granddaughter, Tessa. But it was different. It was a hearing thing. I'm a Deaf person and my story is about growing up Deaf and experiencing the world from a Deaf person's perspective, the Deaf culture view.

### Looking Back

Two things had a big impact on my life: my education in a Deaf school and the fact that I was raised in a hearing family. I look around now and I see many improvements for Deaf people. We have TTY's, telephone relay services, captioned television, the Internet, e-mail, and sign language interpreters in many different places. I see Deaf kids being mainstreamed in public schools with hearing children. But in my heart, I wonder if mainstreaming is the right thing. Maybe the way I did it was better. I had Deaf friends at school and we could communicate and socialize easily with each other. We never needed an interpreter to communicate with our Deaf friends. We all used the same language—ASL.

I don't know what the future holds for Deaf people. I only know that I feel that my education with other Deaf people was right for me. It helped fill the gaps that I missed at home, with my hearing family. The love I got at home taught me how to find places where I could fit in both worlds—of hearing and Deaf people.